# Simple Steps In Qur'ān Reading

## Juz 'Amm

# الخطوة السهلة لقراءة القرآن الكريم

## الجزء عمّ

**Please Note:** Out of respect, because this book contains a complete Juz from the Glorious Qur'ān, all information pages have been placed at the end of the book, after the Qur'ānic text. Please consult these pages before using the book.



Wisdom
PUBLICATIONS

بسم الله الرحمن الرحيم

**In The Name of Allãh,**
**The Most Gracious, The Most Merciful**

# القرآن الكريم

# The Opening

Order in Mushaf: **1**

Order in revelation: **5**

## About the Sûrah

Sûrah al-Fâtihah gets its name from the word al-Fath which means "The Opening", although the word itself does not appear in the Sûrah. The Sûrah is so named because it is the opening chapter of the Qur'ân, and because we open each Raka'ah of Salâh with it. Al-Fâtihah was also the first complete Sûrah of the Qur'ân to be revealed (only a few verses from four other Sûrahs had been revealed before then). Rasûlullâh ﷺ described Sûrah al-Fâtihah as the "Greatest Sûrah in the Qur'ân" and it is also said to summarise the whole Qur'ân.

Sûrah al-Fâtihah is at the heart of our daily prayers; without it no Salâh can be valid; and it is also a du'â, beginning with praise for Allâh ﷻ, before asking for His help and guidance. The rest of the Qur'ân, then, is Allâh's ﷻ answer to that request, providing all the guidance we need.

And lastly, among its many other attributes, Sûrah al-Fâtihah is also a cure for many illnesses.

## Al-Hadîth

Abu Hurayrah رضي الله عنه narrates that Rasûlullâh ﷺ said:

"When, after reciting Sûrah al-Fatihah, the Imâm says âmeen, you should say âmeen too, because the angels also say it, and if anyone's âmeen coincides with the angels' then all his past sins are forgiven."

Source: Al-Bukhârî

سورة الفاتحة

الفاتحة

Ruku': 1

Ayah: 7

أَعُوذُ بِاللّٰهِ مِنَ الشَّيْطَانِ الرَّجِيمِ

بِسْمِ اللّٰهِ الرَّحْمٰنِ الرَّحِيْمِ 1

اَلْحَمْدُ لِلّٰهِ رَبِّ الْعٰلَمِيْنَ 2 اَلرَّحْمٰنِ

الرَّحِيْمِ 3 مٰلِكِ يَوْمِ الدِّيْنِ 4

اِيَّاكَ نَعْبُدُ وَاِيَّاكَ نَسْتَعِيْنُ 5

اِهْدِنَا الصِّرَاطَ الْمُسْتَقِيْمَ 6

صِرَاطَ الَّذِيْنَ اَنْعَمْتَ عَلَيْهِمْ غَيْرِ

الْمَغْضُوْبِ عَلَيْهِمْ وَلَا الضَّآلِّيْنَ 7

Excellent
Good
Repeat

Comments:

I need more help with:
Recognition
Articulation
Fluency

Date Started: / /

Date Completed: / /

مٌّ نّ مّ نْ ـًـ مْ — Read with Ghunnah

ي ُو ـَا ءٓ ــٓ — Read with Madd (stretch)

ي و ا — Silent letters

قْ طْ بْ جْ دْ — Read with Qalqalah (echo)

ظ ط ض ص ق غ خ رُ — Read with velerisation (Full Mouth)

# Section 1

النبأ النازعات

عبس التكوير الإنفطار المطففين

الإنشقاق البروج الطارق

الأعلى الغاشية الفجر البلد

الشمس الليل الضحى

الإنشراح التين العلق القدر

البينة الزلزلة العاديات

القارعة التكاثر العصر الهمزة

الفيل قريش الماعون

الكوثر الكافرون النصر المسد

الإخلاص الفلق الناس

جزء عم

# Juz Amm

The 30th and final Juz of The Glorious Qur'ān

# The News

Order in Mushaf: **78**

Order in revelation: **80**

النبأ

## About the Sūrah

Sūrah an-Nabā' gets its name from the word an-Nabā' meaning "The News" which is found in the second Âyah.

The Sūrah is found at the beginning of the 30th Juz of the Qur'ân and is also known by its first word: 'Am-ma. The name An-Nabā' or "The Announcement/News" refers to the news of the resurrection and the hereafter which forms the principal theme and subject of the Sūrah.

In particular, the Sūrah mentions those who enquire about Yawm al-Qiyāmah (The Day of Judgment), with Allāh ﷻ pointing towards His marvellous creations as evidence that He is capable of doing anything and everything He intends. The Sūrah also reminds us that this world will end one day and another will be established in which every human being from the beginning of time to the end of creation will be resurrected and called to account for their beliefs and deeds.

## Al-Hadīth

Buraidah al-Aslami رضي الله عنه narrates that Rasūlullāh ﷺ said:

"Give glad tidings of light on the Day of Resurrection to those who walk to the Masjid in the dark."

Source: At-Tirmidhī

سورة النبأ

Ruku’: 2 بِسۡمِ اللّٰهِ الرَّحۡمٰنِ الرَّحِيۡمِ Āyah: 40

الجزء Beginning of the Juz



عَمَّ يَتَسَآءَلُوۡنَ ﴿1﴾ عَنِ النَّبَاِ الۡعَظِيۡمِ ﴿2﴾

الَّذِىۡ هُمۡ فِيۡهِ مُخۡتَلِفُوۡنَ ﴿3﴾ كَلَّا

سَيَعۡلَمُوۡنَ ﴿4﴾ ثُمَّ كَلَّا سَيَعۡلَمُوۡنَ ﴿5﴾ اَلَمۡ

نَجۡعَلِ الۡاَرۡضَ مِهٰدًا ﴿6﴾ وَّالۡجِبَالَ

اَوۡتَادًا ﴿7﴾ وَّخَلَقۡنٰكُمۡ اَزۡوَاجًا ﴿8﴾ وَّجَعَلۡنَا

نَوۡمَكُمۡ سُبَاتًا ﴿9﴾ وَّجَعَلۡنَا الَّيۡلَ لِبَاسًا ﴿10﴾

وَّجَعَلۡنَا النَّهَارَ مَعَاشًا ﴿11﴾ وَّبَنَيۡنَا فَوۡقَكُمۡ

سَبۡعًا شِدَادًا ﴿12﴾ وَّجَعَلۡنَا سِرَاجًا وَّهَّاجًا ﴿13﴾

Read with Ghunnah · Read with Madd (stretch) · Silent letters · Read with Qalqalah (echo) · Read with velerisation (Full Mouth)

وَاَنْزَلْنَا مِنَ الْمُعْصِرٰتِ مَآءً ثَجَّاجًا 14
لِّنُخْرِجَ بِهٖ حَبًّا وَّنَبَاتًا 15 وَّجَنّٰتٍ
اَلْفَافًا 16 اِنَّ يَوْمَ الْفَصْلِ كَانَ مِيْقَاتًا 17
يَّوْمَ يُنْفَخُ فِي الصُّوْرِ فَتَاْتُوْنَ اَفْوَاجًا 18
وَّفُتِحَتِ السَّمَآءُ فَكَانَتْ اَبْوَابًا 19 وَّسُيِّرَتِ
الْجِبَالُ فَكَانَتْ سَرَابًا 20 اِنَّ جَهَنَّمَ
كَانَتْ مِرْصَادًا 21 لِّلطَّاغِيْنَ مَاٰبًا 22
لّٰبِثِيْنَ فِيْهَآ اَحْقَابًا 23 لَا يَذُوْقُوْنَ فِيْهَا
بَرْدًا وَّلَا شَرَابًا 24 اِلَّا حَمِيْمًا وَّغَسَّاقًا 25

النبأ

Read with Ghunnah — Read with Madd (stretch) — Silent letters — Read with Qalqalah (echo) — Read with velerisation (Full Mouth)

جَزَآءً وِّفَاقًا ﴿26﴾ اِنَّهُمْ كَانُوْا لَا يَرْجُوْنَ

حِسَابًا ﴿27﴾ وَّكَذَّبُوْا بِاٰيٰتِنَا كِذَّابًا ﴿28﴾ وَكُلَّ

شَيْءٍ اَحْصَيْنٰهُ كِتٰبًا ﴿29﴾ فَذُوْقُوْا فَلَنْ

ع نَّزِيْدَكُمْ اِلَّا عَذَابًا ﴿30﴾ اِنَّ لِلْمُتَّقِيْنَ مَفَازًا

ع 1 30 1

﴿31﴾ حَدَآئِقَ وَاَعْنَابًا ﴿32﴾ وَّكَوَاعِبَ اَتْرَابًا

﴿33﴾ وَّكَاْسًا دِهَاقًا ﴿34﴾ لَا يَسْمَعُوْنَ فِيْهَا

لَغْوًا وَّلَا كِذّٰبًا ﴿35﴾ جَزَآءً مِّنْ رَّبِّكَ عَطَآءً

حِسَابًا ﴿36﴾ رَّبِّ السَّمٰوٰتِ وَالْاَرْضِ وَمَا

بَيْنَهُمَا الرَّحْمٰنِ لَا يَمْلِكُوْنَ مِنْهُ خِطَابًا ﴿37﴾



Read with Ghunnah | Read with Madd (stretch) | Silent letters | Read with Qalqalah (echo) | Read with velerisation (Full Mouth)

يَوْمَ يَقُومُ الرُّوحُ وَالْمَلٰٓئِكَةُ صَفًّا ۖ BETTER to CONTINUE صلے

لَّا يَتَكَلَّمُونَ إِلَّا مَنْ أَذِنَ لَهُ الرَّحْمٰنُ

وَقَالَ صَوَابًا ﴿38﴾ ذٰلِكَ الْيَوْمُ الْحَقُّ ۖ BETTER to CONTINUE صلے

فَمَنْ شَآءَ اتَّخَذَ إِلٰى رَبِّهِ مَاٰبًا ﴿39﴾ إِنَّآ

أَنْذَرْنٰكُمْ عَذَابًا قَرِيبًا يَّوْمَ يَنْظُرُ

الْمَرْءُ مَا قَدَّمَتْ يَدٰهُ وَيَقُولُ الْكَافِرُ

يٰلَيْتَنِي كُنْتُ تُرٰبًا ﴿40﴾ ع

ع 2 10 2

Excellent
Good
Repeat

Comments:

I need more help with:
Recognition
Articulation
Fluency

Date Started: / /
Date Completed: / /

Read with Ghunnah | Read with Madd (stretch) | Silent letters | Read with Qalqalah (echo) | Read with velerisation (Full Mouth)

# (The Angels) Who Extract (Souls)

**Order in Mushaf:** 79

**Order in revelation:** 81

## About the Sûrah

Sûrah an-Nâzi'ât gets its name from the phrase an-Nâzi'âti, which appears in the first Âyah and means "Those Who Extract", referring to the Angels who extract people's souls upon death. The Sûrah describes the fate of good and bad people and opens with oaths sworn upon five characteristics found among the Angels, including the differences in extracting souls from believers and unbelievers, the way these souls are treated after death, and the act of carrying out Allâh's commands swiftly. The Sûrah also mentions those Angels who conduct the affairs of the universe according to Divine Will, and has more references to the Angels than any other Sûrah in the Qur'ân.

As well as describing the roles of the Angels, Sûrah an-Nâzi'ât briefly discusses Yawm al-Qiyâmah (The Day of Judgment) and how those who reject Allâh's message (like most of the Quraish and Fir'awn), will be punished in this life and the next.

*In this book we take the majority view that the oaths in the opening lines of this Sûrah refer to the Angels; there are, however, other interpretations which suggest that the oaths may refer to stars or a combination of stars and angels. This is because the subject of the oaths has not been made clear. And Allâh knows best.

## Al-Hadîth

**Abu Hurayrah narrates that Rasûlullâh said:**

"When the soul of a believer comes out [of its body], two angels receive it and rise with it towards the heavens, whereupon the inhabitants of the heavens say, 'A good soul has come from the Earth. Allâh has blessed you and the body which you used to occupy.' "

**Source: Muslim**

سورة النازعات

Āyah: 46

بِسْمِ اللّٰهِ الرَّحْمٰنِ الرَّحِيْمِ

Ruku': 2

وَالنّٰزِعٰتِ غَرْقًا ﴿1﴾ وَّالنّٰشِطٰتِ نَشْطًا ﴿2﴾

وَّالسّٰبِحٰتِ سَبْحًا ﴿3﴾ فَالسّٰبِقٰتِ سَبْقًا ﴿4﴾

فَالْمُدَبِّرٰتِ اَمْرًا ﴿5﴾ يَوْمَ تَرْجُفُ الرَّاجِفَةُ

﴿6﴾ تَتْبَعُهَا الرَّادِفَةُ ﴿7﴾ قُلُوْبٌ يَّوْمَئِذٍ

وَّاجِفَةٌ ﴿8﴾ اَبْصَارُهَا خَاشِعَةٌ ﴿9﴾ يَقُوْلُوْنَ

ءَاِنَّا لَمَرْدُوْدُوْنَ فِى الْحَافِرَةِ ﴿10﴾ ءَاِذَا كُنَّا

عِظٰمًا نَّخِرَةً ﴿11﴾ قَالُوْا تِلْكَ اِذًا كَرَّةٌ

خَاسِرَةٌ ﴿12﴾ فَاِنَّمَا هِىَ زَجْرَةٌ وَّاحِدَةٌ ﴿13﴾

النازعات

Read with Ghunnah: مّ نّ ن م ن
Read with Madd (stretch): ي و ا ـٓ ـٰ
Silent letters: ا و ي
Read with Qalqalah (echo): ق ط ب ج د
Read with velerisation (Full Mouth): خ غ ق ص ض ط ظ ر

فَإِذَا هُم بِالسَّاهِرَةِ (14) هَلْ أَتَاكَ حَدِيثُ

مُوسَىٰ (15) إِذْ نَادَاهُ رَبُّهُ بِالْوَادِ الْمُقَدَّسِ

طُوًى (16) اذْهَبْ إِلَىٰ فِرْعَوْنَ إِنَّهُ طَغَىٰ (17)

فَقُلْ هَل لَّكَ إِلَىٰ أَن تَزَكَّىٰ (18) وَأَهْدِيَكَ

إِلَىٰ رَبِّكَ فَتَخْشَىٰ (19) فَأَرَاهُ الْآيَةَ الْكُبْرَىٰ

(20) فَكَذَّبَ وَعَصَىٰ (21) ثُمَّ أَدْبَرَ يَسْعَىٰ (22)

فَحَشَرَ فَنَادَىٰ (23) فَقَالَ أَنَا رَبُّكُمُ الْأَعْلَىٰ

(24) فَأَخَذَهُ اللَّهُ نَكَالَ الْآخِرَةِ وَالْأُولَىٰ

(25) إِنَّ فِي ذَٰلِكَ لَعِبْرَةً لِّمَن يَخْشَىٰ (26) ع 1 26 3



Read with Ghunnah | Read with Madd (stretch) | Silent letters | Read with Qalqalah (echo) | Read with velerisation (Full Mouth)

ءَاَنۡتُمۡ اَشَدُّ خَلۡقًا اَمِ السَّمَآءُ ؕ بَنٰهَا ﴿27﴾ رَفَعَ

سَمۡكَهَا فَسَوّٰىهَا ﴿28﴾ وَاَغۡطَشَ لَيۡلَهَا وَاَخۡرَجَ

ضُحٰهَا ﴿29﴾ وَالۡاَرۡضَ بَعۡدَ ذٰلِكَ دَحٰهَا ﴿30﴾

اَخۡرَجَ مِنۡهَا مَآءَهَا وَمَرۡعٰهَا ﴿31﴾ وَالۡجِبَالَ

اَرۡسٰهَا ﴿32﴾ مَتَاعًا لَّكُمۡ وَلِاَنۡعَامِكُمۡ ﴿33﴾

فَاِذَا جَآءَتِ الطَّآمَّةُ الۡكُبۡرٰى ﴿34﴾ يَوۡمَ يَتَذَكَّرُ

الۡاِنۡسَانُ مَا سَعٰى ﴿35﴾ وَبُرِّزَتِ الۡجَحِيۡمُ لِمَنۡ

يَّرٰى ﴿36﴾ فَاَمَّا مَنۡ طَغٰى ﴿37﴾ وَاٰثَرَ الۡحَيٰوةَ

الدُّنۡيَا ﴿38﴾ فَاِنَّ الۡجَحِيۡمَ هِيَ الۡمَاۡوٰى ﴿39﴾

STOP or CONTINUE: ج

Read with Ghunnah: مّ نّ نۡ مۡ
Read with Madd (stretch): ـٓ ا و ي
Silent letters: ا و ي
Read with Qalqalah (echo): ق ط ب ج د
Read with velerisation (Full Mouth): خ ص ض غ ط ق ظ ر

وَاَمَّا مَنْ خَافَ مَقَامَ رَبِّهٖ وَنَهَى النَّفْسَ

عَنِ الْهَوٰى ﴿40﴾ فَاِنَّ الْجَنَّةَ هِيَ الْمَاْوٰى ﴿41﴾

يَسْـَٔلُوْنَكَ عَنِ السَّاعَةِ اَيَّانَ مُرْسٰىهَا ﴿42﴾ فِيْمَ

اَنْتَ مِنْ ذِكْرٰىهَا ﴿43﴾ اِلٰى رَبِّكَ مُنْتَهٰىهَا ﴿44﴾

اِنَّمَآ اَنْتَ مُنْذِرُ مَنْ يَّخْشٰىهَا ﴿45﴾ كَاَنَّهُمْ يَوْمَ

ع 2 30 4 يَرَوْنَهَا لَمْ يَلْبَثُوْٓا اِلَّا عَشِيَّةً اَوْ ضُحٰىهَا ﴿46﴾ ع

79 - Those who Extract

Excellent | Good | Repeat

Comments:

I need more help with: Recognition / Articulation / Fluency

Date Started: / /

Date Completed: / /

Read with Ghunnah: نّ مّ ن مٰ م — Read with Madd (stretch): ي و ا — Silent letters: ي و ا — Read with Qalqalah (echo): ق ط ب ج د — Read with velerisation (Full Mouth): خ غ ق ص ض ط ظ ر

**The Qur'ān states:**

"Indeed the Qur'ān guides to that which is most suitable and gives good tidings to the believers who do righteous deeds that they will have a great reward."

[Qur'ān: 17:9]

# He Frowned

**Order in Mus͟haf:** **80**

**Order in revelation:** **24**

## About the Sûrah

Sûrah 'Abas gets its name from its first word, 'Abasa, which means "He Frowned". In the Sûrah, Allâh ﷻ corrects Rasûlullâh ﷺ for frowning and turning away from a poor blind Sa͟hâbî called 'Abdullâh ibn 'Ummi Maktoum ؓ. Rasûlullâh ﷺ turned away because he was busy meeting with the leaders of the Quraysh (the most important tribe in Makkah), and wanted to end that conversation first, before dealing with 'Abdullâh ؓ. Unaware of this, 'Abdullâh ؓ kept interrupting and while Rasûlullâh ﷺ didn't tell him off, he did frown slightly. Getting upset at being interrupted is human, but as soon as Allâh ﷻ corrected him, (by revealing Sûrah 'Abas), Rasûlullâh ﷺ, left the leaders (whose hearts weren't sincere) and went to speak to 'Abdullâh ؓ, and thereafter was always extra kind to him. Thus Sûrah 'Abas teaches us that sincerity is more important than wealth or status. It does not matter if a person is rich or poor, powerful or weak, able or disabled, male or female, young or old, black or white; Allâh's guidance is for everyone who truly wants it.

## Al-Hadîth

Abu Hurayrah ؓ narrates that Rasûlullâh ﷺ said:

"Verily, Allâh does not look at your appearance or wealth, but rather he looks at your hearts and actions."

Source: Muslim

سورة عبس

Ruku': 1

# بِسۡمِ اللّٰهِ الرَّحۡمٰنِ الرَّحِيۡمِ

Āyah: 42

عَبَسَ وَتَوَلّٰٓى ﴿1﴾ اَنۡ جَآءَهُ الۡاَعۡمٰى ﴿2﴾

وَمَا يُدۡرِيۡكَ لَعَلَّهٗ يَزَّكّٰٓى ﴿3﴾ اَوۡ يَذَّكَّرُ

فَتَنۡفَعَهُ الذِّكۡرٰى ﴿4﴾ اَمَّا مَنِ اسۡتَغۡنٰى ﴿5﴾

فَاَنۡتَ لَهٗ تَصَدّٰى ﴿6﴾ وَمَا عَلَيۡكَ اَلَّا

يَزَّكّٰى ﴿7﴾ وَاَمَّا مَنۡ جَآءَكَ يَسۡعٰى ﴿8﴾ وَهُوَ

يَخۡشٰى ﴿9﴾ فَاَنۡتَ عَنۡهُ تَلَهّٰى ﴿10﴾ كَلَّآ اِنَّهَا

تَذۡكِرَةٌ ﴿11﴾ فَمَنۡ شَآءَ ذَكَرَهٗ ﴿12﴾ فِىۡ

صُحُفٍ مُّكَرَّمَةٍ ﴿13﴾ مَّرۡفُوۡعَةٍ مُّطَهَّرَةٍ ﴿14﴾

Read with Ghunnah | Read with Madd (stretch) | Silent letters | Read with Qalqalah (echo) | Read with velerisation (Full Mouth)

بِاَيۡدِىۡ سَفَرَةٍ ﴿15﴾ كِرَامٍۭ بَرَرَةٍ ﴿16﴾ قُتِلَ

الۡاِنۡسَانُ مَاۤ اَكۡفَرَهٗ ﴿17﴾ مِنۡ اَىِّ شَىۡءٍ

خَلَقَهٗ ﴿18﴾ مِنۡ نُّطۡفَةٍ ؕ خَلَقَهٗ فَقَدَّرَهٗ ﴿19﴾

ثُمَّ السَّبِيۡلَ يَسَّرَهٗ ﴿20﴾ ثُمَّ اَمَاتَهٗ

فَاَقۡبَرَهٗ ﴿21﴾ ثُمَّ اِذَا شَآءَ اَنۡشَرَهٗ ﴿22﴾ كَلَّا لَمَّا

يَقۡضِ مَاۤ اَمَرَهٗ ﴿23﴾ فَلۡيَنۡظُرِ الۡاِنۡسَانُ اِلٰى

طَعَامِهٖۤ ﴿24﴾ اَنَّا صَبَبۡنَا الۡمَآءَ صَبًّا ﴿25﴾ ثُمَّ

شَقَقۡنَا الۡاَرۡضَ شَقًّا ﴿26﴾ فَاَنۡۢبَتۡنَا فِيۡهَا حَبًّا

وَّعِنَبًا وَّقَضۡبًا ﴿27﴾ وَّزَيۡتُوۡنًا وَّنَخۡلًا ﴿28﴾ ﴿29﴾

Read with Ghunnah: مْ نْ مّ نّ
Read with Madd (stretch)
Silent letters: ا و ي
Read with Qalqalah (echo): ق ط ب ج د
Read with velerisation (Full Mouth): خ ص ض غ ط ق ظ ر

عبس

وَحَدَآئِقَ غُلْبًا ﴿30﴾ وَفَاكِهَةً وَّأَبًّا ﴿31﴾ مَّتَاعًا

لَّكُمْ وَلِأَنْعَامِكُمْ ﴿32﴾ فَإِذَا جَآءَتِ الصَّآخَّةُ ﴿33﴾

يَوْمَ يَفِرُّ الْمَرْءُ مِنْ أَخِيهِ ﴿34﴾ وَأُمِّهِ وَأَبِيهِ

﴿35﴾ وَصَاحِبَتِهِ وَبَنِيهِ ﴿36﴾ لِكُلِّ امْرِئٍ مِّنْهُمْ

يَوْمَئِذٍ شَأْنٌ يُغْنِيهِ ﴿37﴾ وُجُوهٌ يَّوْمَئِذٍ

مُّسْفِرَةٌ ﴿38﴾ ضَاحِكَةٌ مُّسْتَبْشِرَةٌ ﴿39﴾ وَوُجُوهٌ

يَّوْمَئِذٍ عَلَيْهَا غَبَرَةٌ ﴿40﴾ تَرْهَقُهَا قَتَرَةٌ ﴿41﴾

أُولَٰٓئِكَ هُمُ الْكَفَرَةُ الْفَجَرَةُ ﴿42﴾ ع 1 42 5

80 - He Frowned

Excellent ◯ | Good ◯ | Repeat ◯

Comments:

I need more help with: Recognition ◯ Articulation ◯ Fluency ◯

Date Started: / /

Date Completed: / /

Read with Ghunnah | Read with Madd (stretch) | Silent letters | Read with Qalqalah (echo) | Read with velerisation (Full Mouth)

# The Folding

Revealed in Makkah

**Order in Mushaf:** 81

**Order in revelation:** 7

## About the Sûrah

Sûrah at-Takweer gets its name from the word kuw-wi-rut, which is found in the first Âyah, and which means "folded" or "wrapped/shrouded". It refers to the moment on Yawm al-Qiyâmah (The Day of Judgement) when the sun will be folded up or shrouded in darkness. The Sûrah provides more details about Yawm al-Qiyâmah than any other Sûrah in the Qur'ân, and is the first of three closely related 'When...' Sûrahs in Juz 'Amm, which give details about that Day using a series of verses starting 'When...', to emphasise that which WILL happen.

Thus Sûrah at-Takweer talks about the opening signs of Qiyâmah, WHEN the sun loses its light, WHEN the stars are scattered and darkened, WHEN the mountains are destroyed, WHEN valuable pregnant she-camels are ignored, WHEN wild animals lose their senses and their fear of each other, WHEN the seas boil, WHEN souls are gathered in like-minded groups, WHEN the records are laid bare, WHEN the skies are stripped away, WHEN hellfire is set ablaze and WHEN heaven is brought near.

## Al-Hadîth

Ibn 'Umar narrates that Rasûlullâh said:

"Whoever wishes to look at the Day of Judgement as if he is seeing it with his own eyes, then let him read [Sûrah at-Takweer, Sûrah al-Infitâr and Sûrah al-Inshiqâq]."

Source: Musnad of Imâm Ahmad

سورة التكوير

Ruku': 1

# بِسۡمِ ٱللَّهِ ٱلرَّحۡمَٰنِ ٱلرَّحِيمِ

Ayah: 29

إِذَا ٱلشَّمۡسُ كُوِّرَتۡ ﴿1﴾ وَإِذَا ٱلنُّجُومُ

ٱنكَدَرَتۡ ﴿2﴾ وَإِذَا ٱلۡجِبَالُ سُيِّرَتۡ ﴿3﴾

وَإِذَا ٱلۡعِشَارُ عُطِّلَتۡ ﴿4﴾ وَإِذَا ٱلۡوُحُوشُ

حُشِرَتۡ ﴿5﴾ وَإِذَا ٱلۡبِحَارُ سُجِّرَتۡ ﴿6﴾ وَإِذَا

ٱلنُّفُوسُ زُوِّجَتۡ ﴿7﴾ وَإِذَا ٱلۡمَوۡءُۥدَةُ

سُئِلَتۡ ﴿8﴾ بِأَيِّ ذَنۢبٖ قُتِلَتۡ ﴿9﴾ وَإِذَا

ٱلصُّحُفُ نُشِرَتۡ ﴿10﴾ وَإِذَا ٱلسَّمَآءُ

كُشِطَتۡ ﴿11﴾ وَإِذَا ٱلۡجَحِيمُ سُعِّرَتۡ ﴿12﴾

81 - The Folding

Read with Ghunnah | Read with Madd (stretch) | Silent letters | Read with Qalqalah (echo) | Read with velerisation (Full Mouth)

وَاِذَا الْجَنَّةُ اُزْلِفَتْ ﴿13﴾ عَلِمَتْ نَفْسٌ

مَّآ اَحْضَرَتْ ﴿14﴾ فَلَآ اُقْسِمُ بِالْخُنَّسِ ﴿15﴾

اَلْجَوَارِ الْكُنَّسِ ﴿16﴾ وَالَّيْلِ اِذَا عَسْعَسَ ﴿17﴾

وَالصُّبْحِ اِذَا تَنَفَّسَ ﴿18﴾ اِنَّهٗ لَقَوْلُ رَسُوْلٍ

كَرِيْمٍ ﴿19﴾ ذِىْ قُوَّةٍ عِنْدَ ذِى الْعَرْشِ

مَكِيْنٍ ﴿20﴾ مُّطَاعٍ ثَمَّ اَمِيْنٍ ﴿21﴾ وَمَا

صَاحِبُكُمْ بِمَجْنُوْنٍ ﴿22﴾ وَلَقَدْ رَاٰهُ بِالْاُفُقِ

الْمُبِيْنِ ﴿23﴾ وَمَا هُوَ عَلَى الْغَيْبِ بِضَنِيْنٍ ﴿24﴾

وَمَا هُوَ بِقَوْلِ شَيْطٰنٍ رَّجِيْمٍ ﴿25﴾

التكوير

Read with Ghunnah: مّ نّ ن مّ ن
Read with Madd (stretch): ي و ا ٓ ٓ
Silent letters: ا و ي
Read with Qalqalah (echo): ق ط ب ج د
Read with velerisation (Full Mouth): خ غ ق ص ض ط ظ رُ

فَأَيْنَ تَذْهَبُونَ ﴿26﴾ إِنْ هُوَ إِلَّا ذِكْرٌ

لِّلْعَٰلَمِينَ ﴿27﴾ لِمَن شَآءَ مِنكُمْ أَن

يَسْتَقِيمَ ﴿28﴾ وَمَا تَشَآءُونَ إِلَّآ أَن

يَشَآءَ ٱللَّهُ رَبُّ ٱلْعَٰلَمِينَ ﴿29﴾ ع

ع 1 29 6

Excellent
Good
Repeat

Comments:

I need more help with:
Recognition
Articulation
Fluency

Date Started: / /

Date Completed: / /

Read with Ghunnah | Read with Madd (stretch) | Silent letters | Read with Qalqalah (echo) | Read with velerisation (Full Mouth)

Once, during his reign as Caliph, some men questioned 'Umar Al-Khattāb ﷺ regarding the leadership of Makkah. The men asked: "Who have you left in charge of Makkah?" He, ﷺ, replied: "Ibn Abzā." They asked: "And who is Ibn Abzā?" 'Umar ﷺ, replied: "A freed slave from those we freed." They remarked: "You left a freed slave in command of the People of the Valley (the noble tribes of the Quraish)?" He ﷺ, replied: "Indeed he is a reciter of the Book of Allāh and is knowledgeable about the obligations of the Muslims. Haven't you heard the statement of your Messenger ﷺ:
'Verily Allāh raises some people by this Book and lowers others by it?'"

Source: Muslim

# The Splitting

Revealed in Makkah

**Order in Mushaf:** 82

**Order in revelation:** 82

## About the Sûrah

Sûrah al-Infitâr gets its name from the word in-fa-ta-rut, found in the first Âyah, which means "split apart" or "break open". This refers to the moment on Yawm al-Qiyâmah (The Day of Judgment) when the sky will split apart. Al-Infitâr is the second of the three 'When...' Sûrahs which give details about Yawm al-Qiyâmah using a series of phrases beginning with 'When...' to emphasise events which will DEFINITELY happen.

As with Sûrah at-Takweer, Sûrah al-Infitâr mentions events which will mark the start of Yawm al-Qiyâmah, namely: WHEN the sky breaks open, WHEN the stars are scattered (meaning the whole cosmic structure will collapse), WHEN the rivers and oceans overflow and submerge the land and WHEN the graves are opened and their occupants resurrected to face judgement. These signs are mentioned as a reminder so that we can prepare for Yawm al-Qiyâmah properly by obeying Allâh ﷻ, and thus gain Jannah (Paradise).

## Al-Hadîth

**Abu Hurayrah ؓ narrates:**

"Rasûlullâh ﷺ said 'Between the two blasts of the trumpet there will be forty.' The people said, 'O Abu Hurayrah! Forty days?' I refused to reply. They said, 'Forty years?' I refused to reply but added: 'Everything of the human body will decay except the tail bone, and from that bone Allâh will reconstruct the whole body.' "

Source: Al-Bukhârî

# سورة الإنفطار

Ruku': 1

بِسۡمِ اللّٰهِ الرَّحۡمٰنِ الرَّحِيۡمِ

Āyah: 19

اِذَا السَّمَآءُ انۡفَطَرَتۡ ﴿1﴾ وَاِذَا الۡكَوَاكِبُ

انۡتَثَرَتۡ ﴿2﴾ وَاِذَا الۡبِحَارُ فُجِّرَتۡ ﴿3﴾

وَاِذَا الۡقُبُوۡرُ بُعۡثِرَتۡ ﴿4﴾ عَلِمَتۡ نَفۡسٌ

مَّا قَدَّمَتۡ وَاَخَّرَتۡ ﴿5﴾ يٰۤاَيُّهَا الۡاِنۡسَانُ

مَا غَرَّكَ بِرَبِّكَ الۡكَرِيۡمِ ﴿6﴾ الَّذِىۡ خَلَقَكَ

فَسَوّٰٮكَ فَعَدَلَكَ ﴿7﴾ فِىۡۤ اَىِّ صُوۡرَةٍ

مَّا شَآءَ رَكَّبَكَ ﴿8﴾ كَلَّا بَلۡ تُكَذِّبُوۡنَ

بِالدِّيۡنِ ﴿9﴾ وَاِنَّ عَلَيۡكُمۡ لَحٰفِظِيۡنَ ﴿10﴾



Read with Ghunnah: مْ ںّ نْ مّ نّ
Read with Madd (stretch)
Silent letters: ا و ي
Read with Qalqalah (echo): قْ طْ بْ جْ دْ
Read with velerisation (Full Mouth): ظ ط ض ص ق غ خ رُ

كِرَامًا كَاتِبِينَ ﴿11﴾ يَعْلَمُونَ مَا تَفْعَلُونَ ﴿12﴾

إِنَّ الْأَبْرَارَ لَفِي نَعِيمٍ ﴿13﴾ وَإِنَّ الْفُجَّارَ

لَفِي جَحِيمٍ ﴿14﴾ يَصْلَوْنَهَا يَوْمَ الدِّينِ ﴿15﴾

وَمَا هُمْ عَنْهَا بِغَائِبِينَ ﴿16﴾ وَمَآ أَدْرَاكَ

مَا يَوْمُ الدِّينِ ﴿17﴾ ثُمَّ مَآ أَدْرَاكَ مَا يَوْمُ

الدِّينِ ﴿18﴾ يَوْمَ لَا تَمْلِكُ نَفْسٌ لِّنَفْسٍ

شَيْئًا صلى BETTER to CONTINUE وَالْأَمْرُ يَوْمَئِذٍ لِّلَّهِ ﴿19﴾ ع

ع 1 19 7

الربع Quarter of the Juz

| Rating | Comments: | I need more help with: | Dates |
| --- | --- | --- | --- |
| Excellent ◯ | | Recognition ◯ | Date Started: / / |
| Good ◯ | | Articulation ◯ | Date Completed: / / |
| Repeat ◯ | | Fluency ◯ | |



مْ نّ مّ نْ مّ — Read with Ghunnah
ي و ا ء ـ — Read with Madd (stretch)
ا و ي — Silent letters
ق ط ب ج د — Read with Qalqalah (echo)
خ ص ض غ ط ق ظ رُ — Read with velerisation (Full Mouth)

# The Cheaters



Revealed in Makkah

Order in Mushaf: **83**

Order in revelation: **86**

## About the Sûrah

Sûrah al-Mutaffifeen gets its name from the word Mutaffifeen found in the first Âyah. The word means “The Cheaters” as the Sûrah condemns those who are dishonest in their dealings and give less, or take more, than is their due. Scholars say that when Rasûlullah ﷺ first moved to Madinah (after the Hijrah), he found merchants in the market using all kinds of tricks to cheat others out of their wealth. In particular, when measuring or weighing goods to give to others they would scrimp and give less than was due, whereas when taking for themselves they would demand the exact amount or take more.

The opening verses of Sûrah al-Mutaffifeen were revealed in response to this and were, in fact, the first verses revealed in Madinah (the rest of the Sûrah, which discusses Yawm al-Qiyâmah, had already been revealed earlier, in Makkah). After these verses were revealed the merchants of Madinah stopped cheating and became known for their honesty.

## Al-Hadîth

’Abdullâh ibn ’Abbâs رضي الله عنه narrates that Rasûlullâh ﷺ said:

**“Those who cheat in measures and weights, Allâh will cause famine to break out amongst them”**

Source: Al-Bazzâr

سورة المطففين

Ruku': 1 بِسۡمِ اللّٰهِ الرَّحۡمٰنِ الرَّحِيۡمِ Āyah: 36

وَيۡلٌ لِّلۡمُطَفِّفِيۡنَ ﴿1﴾ الَّذِيۡنَ اِذَا اكۡتَالُوۡا

عَلَى النَّاسِ يَسۡتَوۡفُوۡنَ ﴿2﴾ وَاِذَا كَالُوۡهُمۡ

اَوۡ وَّزَنُوۡهُمۡ يُخۡسِرُوۡنَ ﴿3﴾ اَلَا يَظُنُّ

اُولٰٓـئِكَ اَنَّهُمۡ مَّبۡعُوۡثُوۡنَ ﴿4﴾ لِيَوۡمٍ عَظِيۡمٍ

﴿5﴾ يَّوۡمَ يَقُوۡمُ النَّاسُ لِرَبِّ الۡعٰلَمِيۡنَ

﴿6﴾ كَلَّاۤ اِنَّ كِتٰبَ الۡفُجَّارِ لَفِىۡ سِجِّيۡنٍ

﴿7﴾ وَمَاۤ اَدۡرٰىكَ مَا سِجِّيۡنٌ ﴿8﴾ كِتٰبٌ

مَّرۡقُوۡمٌ ﴿9﴾ وَيۡلٌ يَّوۡمَئِذٍ لِّلۡمُكَذِّبِيۡنَ ﴿10﴾

Read with Ghunnah | Read with Madd (stretch) | Silent letters | Read with Qalqalah (echo) | Read with velerisation (Full Mouth)

الَّذِينَ يُكَذِّبُونَ بِيَوْمِ الدِّينِ ﴿11﴾ وَمَا

يُكَذِّبُ بِهِۦٓ إِلَّا كُلُّ مُعْتَدٍ أَثِيمٍ ﴿12﴾ إِذَا تُتْلَىٰ

عَلَيْهِ ءَايَٰتُنَا قَالَ أَسَٰطِيرُ الْأَوَّلِينَ ﴿13﴾

كَلَّا ۖ بَلْ ۜ رَانَ عَلَىٰ قُلُوبِهِم مَّا

PAUSE without taking a breath

BETTER to CONTINUE

كَانُوا يَكْسِبُونَ ﴿14﴾ كَلَّآ إِنَّهُمْ عَن رَّبِّهِمْ

يَوْمَئِذٍ لَّمَحْجُوبُونَ ﴿15﴾ ثُمَّ إِنَّهُمْ لَصَالُوا

الْجَحِيمِ ﴿16﴾ ثُمَّ يُقَالُ هَٰذَا الَّذِى كُنتُم

بِهِۦ تُكَذِّبُونَ ﴿17﴾ كَلَّآ إِنَّ كِتَٰبَ الْأَبْرَارِ

لَفِى عِلِّيِّينَ ﴿18﴾ وَمَآ أَدْرَىٰكَ مَا عِلِّيُّونَ ﴿19﴾

Read with Ghunnah | Read with Madd (stretch) | Silent letters | Read with Qalqalah (echo) | Read with velerisation (Full Mouth)

المطففين

كِتَٰبٌ مَّرْقُومٌ 20 يَشْهَدُهُ ٱلْمُقَرَّبُونَ 21

إِنَّ ٱلْأَبْرَارَ لَفِى نَعِيمٍ 22 عَلَى ٱلْأَرَآئِكِ

يَنظُرُونَ 23 تَعْرِفُ فِى وُجُوهِهِمْ نَضْرَةَ

ٱلنَّعِيمِ 24 يُسْقَوْنَ مِن رَّحِيقٍ مَّخْتُومٍ 25

خِتَٰمُهُۥ مِسْكٌ ج وَفِى ذَٰلِكَ فَلْيَتَنَافَسِ

STOP or CONTINUE

ٱلْمُتَنَٰفِسُونَ 26 وَمِزَاجُهُۥ مِن تَسْنِيمٍ 27

عَيْنًا يَشْرَبُ بِهَا ٱلْمُقَرَّبُونَ 28 إِنَّ ٱلَّذِينَ

أَجْرَمُوا۟ كَانُوا۟ مِنَ ٱلَّذِينَ ءَامَنُوا۟ يَضْحَكُونَ

29 وَإِذَا مَرُّوا۟ بِهِمْ يَتَغَامَزُونَ 30

Read with Ghunnah · Read with Madd (stretch) · Silent letters · Read with Qalqalah (echo) · Read with velerisation (Full Mouth)

وَإِذَا انقَلَبُوٓا إِلَىٰٓ أَهۡلِهِمُ انقَلَبُوا فَكِهِينَ

31 وَإِذَا رَأَوۡهُمۡ قَالُوٓا إِنَّ هَٰٓؤُلَآءِ لَضَآلُّونَ

32 وَمَآ أُرۡسِلُوا عَلَيۡهِمۡ حَٰفِظِينَ 33

فَٱلۡيَوۡمَ ٱلَّذِينَ ءَامَنُوا مِنَ ٱلۡكُفَّارِ

يَضۡحَكُونَ 34 عَلَى ٱلۡأَرَآئِكِ يَنظُرُونَ 35

ع 36 هَلۡ ثُوِّبَ ٱلۡكُفَّارُ مَا كَانُوا يَفۡعَلُونَ

ع 1 36 8

Excellent
Good
Repeat

Comments:

I need more help with:
Recognition
Articulation
Fluency

Date Started: / /
Date Completed: / /

مۡ | نّ | نۡ | مّ | نّ — Read with Ghunnah
ـآ | ـٓ | ـا | ـو | ـي — Read with Madd (stretch)
ا | و | ي — Silent letters
قۡ | طۡ | بۡ | جۡ | دۡ — Read with Qalqalah (echo)
ظ | ط | ض | ص | ق | غ | خ | رُ — Read with velerisation (Full Mouth)

مَا شَاءَ اللّٰه
You have just learnt another Sûrah from Al-Qur'ān

Don't forget to mark off on the progress sheet!

# The Tearing

**Order in Mushaf:** 84

**Order in revelation:** 83

## About the Sûrah

Sûrah al-Inshiqâq gets its name from the word in-shaq-qat, meaning "to tear apart", which is found in the first Âyah, and refers to the tearing apart of the sky at the start of Yawm al-Qiyâmah (The Day of Judgement). Al-Inshiqâq is the third of the three closely related 'When...' Sûrahs which describe the events of Qiyâmah using a series of phrases beginning with 'When...'. It continues the themes of the previous Sûrahs by describing two events that will take place at the start of Yawm al-Qiyâmah, namely: WHEN the sky is torn apart and WHEN the Earth is flattened and emptied of all it contains, including both natural treasures and bodies from their graves.

The Sûrah then describes a key moment of Yawm al-Qiyâmah when each person will receive their Book of Deeds; those who receive it in their right hands will be successful in the hereafter, whereas those who receive it behind their backs will be unsuccessful.

## Al-Hadîth

**Abu-Salamah ﵁ narrates:**

"While leading them in prayer, Abu-Hurayrah ﵁ recited [Sûrah al-Inshiqâq] and prostrated during its recitation. After he completed the prayer, he informed his companions that Rasûlullâh ﷺ prostrated during its recitation."

**Source: Muslim**

## سورة الإنشقاق

Ruku': 1

بِسْمِ اللّٰهِ الرَّحْمٰنِ الرَّحِيْمِ

Āyah: 25

اِذَا السَّمَآءُ انْشَقَّتْ 1 وَاَذِنَتْ لِرَبِّهَا
وَحُقَّتْ 2 وَاِذَا الْاَرْضُ مُدَّتْ 3 وَاَلْقَتْ
مَا فِيْهَا وَتَخَلَّتْ 4 وَاَذِنَتْ لِرَبِّهَا وَحُقَّتْ
5 يٰاَيُّهَا الْاِنْسَانُ اِنَّكَ كَادِحٌ اِلٰى
رَبِّكَ كَدْحًا فَمُلٰقِيْهِ 6 فَاَمَّا مَنْ اُوْتِيَ
كِتٰبَهٗ بِيَمِيْنِهٖ 7 فَسَوْفَ يُحَاسَبُ حِسَابًا
يَّسِيْرًا 8 وَيَنْقَلِبُ اِلٰى اَهْلِهٖ مَسْرُوْرًا 9
وَاَمَّا مَنْ اُوْتِيَ كِتٰبَهٗ وَرَآءَ ظَهْرِهٖ 10

Read with Ghunnah: مْ نّ مّ نْ ںّ ںْ

Read with Madd (stretch): ىٓ ـًا ـُو ـِي

Silent letters: ا و ي

Read with Qalqalah (echo): قْ طْ بْ جْ دْ

Read with velerisation (Full Mouth): خ غ ق ص ض ط ظ رُ

فَسَوۡفَ يَدۡعُوا۟ ثُبُورٗا 11 وَيَصۡلَىٰ سَعِيرًا

12 إِنَّهُۥ كَانَ فِيٓ أَهۡلِهِۦ مَسۡرُورًا 13 إِنَّهُۥ

ظَنَّ أَن لَّن يَحُورَ 14 بَلَىٰٓۚ إِنَّ رَبَّهُۥ كَانَ بِهِۦ

بَصِيرٗا 15 فَلَآ أُقۡسِمُ بِٱلشَّفَقِ 16 وَٱلَّيۡلِ

وَمَا وَسَقَ 17 وَٱلۡقَمَرِ إِذَا ٱتَّسَقَ 18

لَتَرۡكَبُنَّ طَبَقًا عَن طَبَقٖ 19 فَمَا لَهُمۡ

لَا يُؤۡمِنُونَ 20 وَإِذَا قُرِئَ عَلَيۡهِمُ ٱلۡقُرۡءَانُ

لَا يَسۡجُدُونَ ۩ 21 بَلِ ٱلَّذِينَ كَفَرُوا۟

السجدة

Perform a Prostration

يُكَذِّبُونَ 22 وَٱللَّهُ أَعۡلَمُ بِمَا يُوعُونَ 23

Prostration

الإنشقاق

Read with Ghunnah
Read with Madd (stretch)
Silent letters
Read with Qalqalah (echo)
Read with velerisation (Full Mouth)

فَبَشِّرْهُمْ بِعَذَابٍ اَلِيْمٍ 24 اِلَّا الَّذِيْنَ اٰمَنُوْا

وَعَمِلُوا الصّٰلِحٰتِ لَهُمْ اَجْرٌ غَيْرُ مَمْنُوْنٍ 25 ع

ع 1 25 9



| | | | |
|---|---|---|---|
| Excellent | Comments: | I need more help with: | Date Started: / / |
| Good | | Recognition | |
| Repeat | | Articulation | Date Completed: / / |
| | | Fluency | |

Read with Ghunnah · Read with Madd (stretch) · Silent letters · Read with Qalqalah (echo) · Read with velerisation (Full Mouth)

This Sûrah is one in which Rasûlullâh ﷺ used to make Sajdah at-Tilâwah (prostration of recitation - i.e. place the knees, hands and forehead on the ground, like we do in the five daily prayers).

In Âyah 21 Allâh ﷻ says that the disbelievers do not make Sajdah when the Qur'ân is recited. Therefore, Rasûlullâh ﷺ used to make Sajdah when he recited this verse, to show that Muslims are different from the disbelievers. Believers make Sajdah to show their obedience to Allâh ﷻ in all things, like reading a verse from the Qur'ân. There are 14/15 places in the Qur'ân when we make Sajdah at-Tilâwah, and each is marked by a line over the word "as-Sajdah" in the text and/or a symbol at the end of the Âyah, as in the 21st Âyah of this Sûrah.

**(Optional) Du'â when making Sajdah at-Tilâwah (prostrating)**

اَللّٰهُمَّ لَكَ سَجَدْتُّ وَبِكَ اٰمَنْتُ ، وَلَكَ اَسْلَمْتُ ،

O Allâh, unto You I have prostrated and in You I have believed, and unto You I have submitted.

سَجَدَ وَجْهِيَ لِلَّذِيْ خَلَقَهٗ وَصَوَّرَهٗ وَشَقَّ سَمْعَهٗ وَبَصَرَهٗ ،

My face has prostrated before He Who created it and fashioned it, and brought forth its faculties of hearing and seeing.

بِحَوْلِهٖ وَقُوَّتِهٖ تَبَارَكَ اللّٰهُ اَحْسَنُ الْخَالِقِيْنَ

Blessed is Allâh, the best of creators.

Sources: Muslim, Abu-Dâ'wûd, At-Tirmidhî, An-Nasâ'î and Ibn Mâjah

# The Constellations

Order in Mushaf: **85**

Order in revelation: **27**



## About the Sûrah

Sûrah al-Burûj gets its name from the word Al-Burûj, which is found in the first Âyah, and means "The Constellations". The Sûrah serves as both a warning and a promise and begins with Allâh ﷻ taking an oath by the sky and its constellations. He then mentions a past nation of people called As-hâbul-ukhdûd, The People of the Ditch, who persecuted those who believed in Allâh ﷻ. The king of the nation ordered all those who believed in Allâh ﷻ to renounce their faith. When they refused, the king became so angry that he threw them into a ditch and harmed them in a most cruel and savage way.

In Sûrah al-Burûj Allâh ﷻ warns those who harm His servants that they will have to face the consequences of their actions in both this life and the hereafter. And Allâh ﷻ also promises those believers who remain patient during great difficulties, and hold steadfast to their faith, that they will be rewarded.

## Al-Hadîth

**Abu Hurayrah ﷺ narrates that Rasûlullâh ﷺ said:**

"The example of a believer is that of a fresh tender plant. From whatever direction the wind comes, the plant bends; and then straightens again when the wind dies down. Similarly, when a believer is afflicted with calamities [he remains patient until Allâh removes his difficulties]. Whereas an impious person is like a pine tree which keeps hard and straight [and doesn't bend with the wind] until Allâh brings it down [e.g with a storm]."

Source: Al-Bukhârî

# سورة البروج

Ruku': 1

بِسْمِ اللّٰهِ الرَّحْمٰنِ الرَّحِيْمِ

Āyah: 22

وَالسَّمَآءِ ذَاتِ الْبُرُوْجِ 1 وَالْيَوْمِ

الْمَوْعُوْدِ 2 وَشَاهِدٍ وَّمَشْهُوْدٍ 3 قُتِلَ

اَصْحٰبُ الْاُخْدُوْدِ 4 النَّارِ ذَاتِ الْوَقُوْدِ

5 اِذْ هُمْ عَلَيْهَا قُعُوْدٌ 6 وَّهُمْ عَلٰى مَا

يَفْعَلُوْنَ بِالْمُؤْمِنِيْنَ شُهُوْدٌ 7 وَمَا

نَقَمُوْا مِنْهُمْ اِلَّآ اَنْ يُّؤْمِنُوْا بِاللّٰهِ الْعَزِيْزِ

الْحَمِيْدِ 8 الَّذِىْ لَهٗ مُلْكُ السَّمٰوٰتِ

وَالْاَرْضِ ج وَاللّٰهُ عَلٰى كُلِّ شَىْءٍ شَهِيْدٌ 9

STOP or CONTINUE

85 - The Constellations

Read with Ghunnah
Read with Madd (stretch)
Silent letters
Read with Qalqalah (echo)
Read with velerisation (Full Mouth)

إِنَّ الَّذِيْنَ فَتَنُوا الْمُؤْمِنِيْنَ وَالْمُؤْمِنٰتِ

ثُمَّ لَمْ يَتُوْبُوْا فَلَهُمْ عَذَابُ جَهَنَّمَ وَلَهُمْ

عَذَابُ الْحَرِيْقِ 10 إِنَّ الَّذِيْنَ اٰمَنُوْا وَعَمِلُوا

الصّٰلِحٰتِ لَهُمْ جَنّٰتٌ تَجْرِيْ مِنْ تَحْتِهَا

الْاَنْهٰرُ ج ذٰلِكَ الْفَوْزُ الْكَبِيْرُ 11 إِنَّ بَطْشَ

STOP or CONTINUE

رَبِّكَ لَشَدِيْدٌ 12 إِنَّهٗ هُوَ يُبْدِئُ وَيُعِيْدُ 13

وَهُوَ الْغَفُوْرُ الْوَدُوْدُ 14 ذُو الْعَرْشِ

الْمَجِيْدُ 15 فَعَّالٌ لِّمَا يُرِيْدُ 16 هَلْ اَتٰىكَ

حَدِيْثُ الْجُنُوْدِ 17 فِرْعَوْنَ وَثَمُوْدَ 18

البروج

Read with Ghunnah | Read with Madd (stretch) | Silent letters | Read with Qalqalah (echo) | Read with velerisation (Full Mouth)

بَلِ الَّذِينَ كَفَرُوا فِي تَكْذِيبٍ ﴿١٩﴾ وَاللَّهُ
19
مِن وَرَآئِهِم مُّحِيطٌ ﴿٢٠﴾ بَلْ هُوَ قُرْآنٌ
20
مَّجِيدٌ ﴿٢١﴾ فِي لَوْحٍ مَّحْفُوظٍ ﴿٢٢﴾
21
22

Excellent
Good
Repeat

Comments:

I need more help with:
Recognition
Articulation
Fluency

Date Started: / /

Date Completed: / /



Read with Ghunnah: نّ مّ ن م
Read with Madd (stretch): ي و ا
Silent letters: ا و ي
Read with Qalqalah (echo): ق ط ب ج د
Read with velerisation (Full Mouth): ظ ط ض ص ق غ خ ر

مَا شَاءَ اللّٰه
You have just learnt another Sūrah from Al-Qur'ān

Don't forget to mark off on the progress sheet!

'Uqbah ibn 'Âmir said: "Rasûlullāh came to us while we were sitting on the Suffa and asked if anyone of us would like to go to the market of Buthān or Aqeeq and fetch from there two she-camels of the finest breed without committing any sin or severing a tie of kinship. We replied that every one of us would love to do so. Rasûlullāh then said that going to the Masjid and reciting or teaching two Âyahs (verses) of the Qur'ān is more precious than two she-camels, three Âyahs are more precious than three she-camels, and that similarly reciting or teaching of four Âyahs is better than four she-camels and so forth."

Source: Muslim

# The Night Visitor

**Order in Mushaf:** 86

**Order in revelation:** 36

## About the Sûrah

Sûrah at-Târiq gets its name from the word At-Târiq, found in the first Âyah, meaning "The Night Visitor". The phrase refers to a bright star which appears like a visitor in the sky during the darkest part of the night, to watch over us like a guardian. Sûrah at-Târiq reminds us that our actions are indeed being watched and recorded throughout our lives, by Angels that Allâh ﷻ has appointed as watchers and guardians over every human being. Their role is both to record our deeds and actions, and to protect us from calamities (as Allâh ﷻ commands and accepting those things He has decreed to happen). The Sûrah also reminds us that on Yawm al-Qiyâmah (The Day of Judgement), when we are most in need of help and guardians, we will have no helpers except as Allâh ﷻ decrees. Inshâ' Allâh, if we read the Qur'ân regularly, understand its message and act upon its teachings, then the Qur'ân itself will act as a helper and guardian for us on that Day.

## Al-Hadîth

'Abdullâh ibn Mas'ood ؓ narrates that Rasûlullâh ﷺ said:

"The Qur'ân is an intercessor (something given permission to intercede), and it is rightfully believed in. Whoever puts it in front of him, it will lead him to Paradise; whoever puts it behind him, it will steer him to the Hellfire."

Source: At-Tabarânî

الطارق

# سورة الطارق

Ruku': 1

بِسۡمِ اللّٰهِ الرَّحۡمٰنِ الرَّحِيۡمِ

Âyah: 17

وَالسَّمَآءِ وَالطَّارِقِ ﴿1﴾ وَمَآ اَدۡرٰىكَ

مَا الطَّارِقُ ﴿2﴾ اَلنَّجۡمُ الثَّاقِبُ ﴿3﴾ اِنۡ

كُلُّ نَفۡسٍ لَّمَّا عَلَيۡهَا حَافِظٌ ﴿4﴾ فَلۡيَنۡظُرِ

الۡاِنۡسَانُ مِمَّ خُلِقَ ﴿5﴾ خُلِقَ مِنۡ مَّآءٍ

دَافِقٍ ﴿6﴾ يَّخۡرُجُ مِنۡۢ بَيۡنِ الصُّلۡبِ

وَالتَّرَآئِبِ ﴿7﴾ اِنَّهٗ عَلٰى رَجۡعِهٖ لَقَادِرٌ ﴿8﴾

يَوۡمَ تُبۡلَى السَّرَآئِرُ ﴿9﴾ فَمَا لَهٗ مِنۡ قُوَّةٍ

وَّلَا نَاصِرٍ ﴿10﴾ وَالسَّمَآءِ ذَاتِ الرَّجۡعِ ﴿11﴾

86 - The Night Vistior

Read with Ghunnah | Read with Madd (stretch) | Silent letters | Read with Qalqalah (echo) | Read with velerisation (Full Mouth)

وَالْاَرْضِ ذَاتِ الصَّدْعِ ﴿12﴾ اِنَّهٗ لَقَوْلٌ

فَصْلٌ ﴿13﴾ وَّمَا هُوَ بِالْهَزْلِ ﴿14﴾ اِنَّهُمْ

يَكِيْدُوْنَ كَيْدًا ﴿15﴾ وَّاَكِيْدُ كَيْدًا ﴿16﴾

فَمَهِّلِ الْكٰفِرِيْنَ اَمْهِلْهُمْ رُوَيْدًا ﴿17﴾ ع

ع 1 17 11

Excellent | Good | Repeat

Comments:

I need more help with: Recognition / Articulation / Fluency

Date Started: / /

Date Completed: / /



Read with Ghunnah — Read with Madd (stretch) — Silent letters — Read with Qalqalah (echo) — Read with velerisation (Full Mouth)

**Jābir ﷺ narrates:**
**"Mu'ādh ﷺ lead the Maghrib prayer and recited Sūrahs Al-Baqarah and An-Nisā [two very long Sūrahs] Rasūlullāh ﷺ said to him: "Are you putting the people to trial, O Mu'ādh ﷺ? Was it not sufficient for you to recite Was-Samā'i wat-Țāriq (Sūrah at-Țāriq) and Wash Shamsi wa Duhāha (Sūrah ash-Shams), or something like them?"**
**Source: An-Nasā'ī**

# The Most High

**Order in Mushaf:** 87

**Order in revelation:** 8

## About the Sûrah

Sûrah al-'A'lâ gets its name from the word Al-'A'lâ, meaning "The Most High", which is used in the first Âyah.
This Sûrah is all about the greatness of Allâh ﷻ and reminds us that we need to glorify and praise Him because of all the many blessings He has given us and the careful plan He has made for His creation. The Sûrah also mentions how Allâh ﷻ has repeated this message to people throughout history, including in the earlier revelations of Sayyidinah Ibrahîm ؑ and Musâ ؑ.

Upon reading the first Âyah of Sûrah al-'A'lâ, Rasûlullâh ﷺ used to recite the words

سُبْحَٰنَ رَبِّيَ الْأَعْلَىٰ

"Glory to my Lord, the Most High"
Which served further to emphasise the greatness of Allâh ﷻ. This is a sunnah (custom) of Rasûlullâh ﷺ which we should all try to make part of our own practice.

## Al-Hadîth

Ibn 'Abbâs ؓ narrates:

Rasûlullâh ﷺ used to recite Sûrah al-'A'lâ in the first Raka'ah of the Witr prayer, followed by Sûrah al-Kâfiroon and Sûrah al-Ikhlâs in the subsequent two Raka'ah.

Source: Musnad of Imâm Ahmad

سورة الأعلى

Ruku': 1

بِسۡمِ اللّٰهِ الرَّحۡمٰنِ الرَّحِيۡمِ

Āyah: 19

سَبِّحِ اسۡمَ رَبِّكَ الۡاَعۡلَى ۝١ الَّذِىۡ خَلَقَ

فَسَوّٰى ۝٢ وَالَّذِىۡ قَدَّرَ فَهَدٰى ۝٣ وَالَّذِىۡۤ

اَخۡرَجَ الۡمَرۡعٰى ۝٤ فَجَعَلَهٗ غُثَآءً اَحۡوٰى ۝٥

سَنُقۡرِئُكَ فَلَا تَنۡسٰٓى ۝٦ اِلَّا مَا شَآءَ اللّٰهُ ؕ ج

STOP or CONTINUE

اِنَّهٗ يَعۡلَمُ الۡجَهۡرَ وَمَا يَخۡفٰى ۝٧ وَنُيَسِّرُكَ

لِلۡيُسۡرٰى ۝٨ فَذَكِّرۡ اِنۡ نَّفَعَتِ الذِّكۡرٰى ۝٩

سَيَذَّكَّرُ مَنۡ يَّخۡشٰى ۝١٠ وَيَتَجَنَّبُهَا الۡاَشۡقَى

الَّذِىۡ يَصۡلَى النَّارَ الۡكُبۡرٰى ۝١١ ۝١٢

سَبِّحِ اسْمَ رَبِّكَ الْأَعْلَى

الأعلى

Read with Ghunnah: مْ نّ نْ مّ نّ

Read with Madd (stretch)

Silent letters: ا و ي

Read with Qalqalah (echo): ق ط ب ج د

Read with velerisation (Full Mouth): ظ ط ض ص ق غ خ رُ

ثُمَّ لَا يَمُوتُ فِيهَا وَلَا يَحْيٰى 13 قَدْ اَفْلَحَ

مَنْ تَزَكّٰى 14 وَذَكَرَ اسْمَ رَبِّهٖ فَصَلّٰى 15

بَلْ تُؤْثِرُونَ الْحَيٰوةَ الدُّنْيَا 16 وَالْاٰخِرَةُ

خَيْرٌ وَّاَبْقٰى 17 اِنَّ هٰذَا لَفِي الصُّحُفِ

الْاُولٰى 18 صُحُفِ اِبْرٰهِيمَ وَمُوسٰى 19

Excellent
Good
Repeat

Comments:

I need more help with:
Recognition
Articulation
Fluency

Date Started: / /
Date Completed: / /

Read with Ghunnah: مّ نّ ن مْ
Read with Madd (stretch): ا و ي
Silent letters: ا و ي
Read with Qalqalah (echo): ق ط ب ج د
Read with velerisation (Full Mouth): خ ص ض غ ط ق ظ ر



مَا شَاءَ اللّٰه
You have just learnt another Sūrah from Al-Qur'ān

Don't forget to mark off on the progress sheet!

**'Abdullāh bin 'Abbās ﷺ narrates:**

"The Prophet ﷺ used to recite in the 'Eid prayer 'Glorify the Name of your Lord, the Most High.' [Al-'A'lā (87)] and 'Has there come to you the narration of the overwhelming?' [Al-Ghāshiyah (88)]"

**Source: Ibn Mājah**

# An Overwhelming Event

**Order in Mushaf:** 88

**Order in revelation:** 68

## About the Sûrah

Sûrah al-Ghâshiyah gets its name from the word Ghâshiyah, meaning "An Overwhelming Event" which is used in the first Âyah. Al-Ghâshiyah is another name for Yawm al-Qiyâmah (the Day of Judgment) and the Sûrah discusses various aspects of that Day. It begins by describing how people's faces on Yawm al-Qiyâmah will be happy or sad depending on whether they are successful or unsuccessful - this being determined by the efforts they made to obey Allâh ﷻ during their lives.

Then, after mentioning the condition of the unsuccessful, Allâh ﷻ goes on to give some details about Jannah, where the successful people will go. It is described as a place where there will be no unpleasant speech or sights, but only pleasant surroundings and words of peace; a place of flowing springs and high thrones to sit on, with cups set in place ready for serving drinks; and a place with soft pillows in neat rows to rest upon, and beautiful, soft carpets spread out on the ground.

## Al-Hadîth

An-Nu'mân bin Bashîr رضي الله عنه narrates:

"Rasûlullâh ﷺ used to recite Sûrah al-'A'lâ and Sûrah al-Ghâshiyah in the 'Eid and Jumu'ah prayers."

Source: Muslim

سورة الغاشية

Ruku': 1 بِسۡمِ اللّٰهِ الرَّحۡمٰنِ الرَّحِيۡمِ Āyah: 26

هَلۡ اَتٰىكَ حَدِيۡثُ الۡغَاشِيَةِ 1 وُجُوۡهٌ

يَّوۡمَئِذٍ خَاشِعَةٌ 2 عَامِلَةٌ نَّاصِبَةٌ 3 تَصۡلٰى

نَارًا حَامِيَةً 4 تُسۡقٰى مِنۡ عَيۡنٍ اٰنِيَةٍ 5

لَّيۡسَ لَهُمۡ طَعَامٌ اِلَّا مِنۡ ضَرِيۡعٍ 6 لَّا يُسۡمِنُ

وَلَا يُغۡنِىۡ مِنۡ جُوۡعٍ 7 وُّجُوۡهٌ يَّوۡمَئِذٍ نَّاعِمَةٌ

لِّسَعۡيِهَا رَاضِيَةٌ 8 فِىۡ جَنَّةٍ عَالِيَةٍ 9 10

لَّا تَسۡمَعُ فِيۡهَا لَاغِيَةً 11 فِيۡهَا عَيۡنٌ جَارِيَةٌ 12

فِيۡهَا سُرُرٌ مَّرۡفُوۡعَةٌ 13 وَّاَكۡوَابٌ مَّوۡضُوۡعَةٌ 14

88 - The Overwhelming Event

Read with Ghunnah | Read with Madd (stretch) | Silent letters | Read with Qalqalah (echo) | Read with velerisation (Full Mouth)

وَّنَمَارِقُ مَصۡفُوۡفَةٌ ﴿15﴾ وَّزَرَابِیُّ مَبۡثُوۡثَةٌ ﴿16﴾

اَفَلَا یَنۡظُرُوۡنَ اِلَی الۡاِبِلِ کَیۡفَ خُلِقَتۡ ﴿17﴾

وَاِلَی السَّمَآءِ کَیۡفَ رُفِعَتۡ ﴿18﴾ وَاِلَی الۡجِبَالِ

کَیۡفَ نُصِبَتۡ ﴿19﴾ وَاِلَی الۡاَرۡضِ کَیۡفَ

سُطِحَتۡ ﴿20﴾ فَذَکِّرۡ اِنَّمَاۤ اَنۡتَ مُذَکِّرٌ ﴿21﴾ لَسۡتَ

عَلَیۡهِمۡ بِمُصَیۡطِرٍ ﴿22﴾ اِلَّا مَنۡ تَوَلّٰی وَکَفَرَ

﴿23﴾ فَیُعَذِّبُهُ اللّٰهُ الۡعَذَابَ الۡاَکۡبَرَ ﴿24﴾ اِنَّ

1 ع 26 13

ع

اِلَیۡنَاۤ اِیَابَهُمۡ ﴿25﴾ ثُمَّ اِنَّ عَلَیۡنَا حِسَابَهُمۡ ﴿26﴾

الغاشية

النصف Half of the Juz

Excellent

Good

Repeat

Comments:

I need more help with:

Recognition

Articulation

Fluency

Date Started: / /

Date Completed: / /

Read with Ghunnah | Read with Madd (stretch) | Silent letters | Read with Qalqalah (echo) | Read with velerisation (Full Mouth)

# The Dawn

**Order in Mushaf:** 89

**Order in revelation:** 10

## About the Sûrah

Sûrah al-Fajr gets its name from the word Al-Fajr, meaning "The Dawn" which is used in the first Âyah. This Sûrah is another which starts with Allâh ﷻ taking multiple oaths, in this case upon:

i) The Dawn, which could refer to the dawn in general or the dawn of a particular day such as the 1st of Muharram (the first day of the lunar year) or the 10th of Dhul Hijjah (the only day which has no associated night).

ii) The Ten Nights, which could refer to the first ten nights of Dhul Hijjah, or the last ten nights of Ramadhân.

iii) The Even and the Odd, which could refer to the arrangement of even and odd things in creation, or the even and odd number of Raka'ah in Salâh or certain special nights of the year such as the 9th and 10th of Dhul Hijjah.

iv) The Passing of Night, which could refer both to daybreak or to illumination following darkness in general, such as knowledge following ignorance.

## Al-Hadîth

Ibn 'Abbâs رضي الله عنه narrates that Rasûlullâh ﷺ said:

"There are no days in which righteous deeds are more beloved to Allâh ﷻ then [the first Ten Days of Dhul Hijjah]..."

Source: Al-Bukhârî

سورة الفجر

Ruku': 1

بِسۡمِ اللّٰهِ الرَّحۡمٰنِ الرَّحِيۡمِ

Āyah: 30

وَالۡفَجۡرِ ﴿1﴾ وَلَيَالٍ عَشۡرٍ ﴿2﴾ وَّالشَّفۡعِ

وَالۡوَتۡرِ ﴿3﴾ وَالَّيۡلِ اِذَا يَسۡرِ ﴿4﴾ هَلۡ فِىۡ

ذٰلِكَ قَسَمٌ لِّذِىۡ حِجۡرٍ ﴿5﴾ اَلَمۡ تَرَ كَيۡفَ

فَعَلَ رَبُّكَ بِعَادٍ ﴿6﴾ اِرَمَ ذَاتِ الۡعِمَادِ ﴿7﴾

الَّتِىۡ لَمۡ يُخۡلَقۡ مِثۡلُهَا فِى الۡبِلَادِ ﴿8﴾

وَثَمُوۡدَ الَّذِيۡنَ جَابُوا الصَّخۡرَ بِالۡوَادِ ﴿9﴾

وَفِرۡعَوۡنَ ذِى الۡاَوۡتَادِ ﴿10﴾ الَّذِيۡنَ طَغَوۡا

فِى الۡبِلَادِ ﴿11﴾ فَاَكۡثَرُوۡا فِيۡهَا الۡفَسَادَ ﴿12﴾

Read with Ghunnah: مّ نّ نۡ ـً مۡ

Read with Madd (stretch): ىٓ ـٰ ـٗ ـا ـٖ وِ ي

Silent letters: ا و ي

Read with Qalqalah (echo): ق ط ب ج د

Read with velerisation (Full Mouth): ظ ط ض ص ق غ خ رُ

فَصَبَّ عَلَيۡهِمۡ رَبُّكَ سَوۡطَ عَذَابٍ 13 إِنَّ

رَبَّكَ لَبِالۡمِرۡصَادِ 14 فَأَمَّا ٱلۡإِنسَٰنُ إِذَا مَا

ٱبۡتَلَىٰهُ رَبُّهُۥ فَأَكۡرَمَهُۥ وَنَعَّمَهُۥ فَيَقُولُ رَبِّيٓ

أَكۡرَمَنِ 15 وَأَمَّآ إِذَا مَا ٱبۡتَلَىٰهُ فَقَدَرَ عَلَيۡهِ

رِزۡقَهُۥ فَيَقُولُ رَبِّيٓ أَهَٰنَنِ 16 كَلَّا ۖ بَل لَّا

تُكۡرِمُونَ ٱلۡيَتِيمَ 17 وَلَا تَحَٰٓضُّونَ عَلَىٰ

طَعَامِ ٱلۡمِسۡكِينِ 18 وَتَأۡكُلُونَ ٱلتُّرَاثَ

أَكۡلٗا لَّمّٗا 19 وَتُحِبُّونَ ٱلۡمَالَ حُبّٗا جَمّٗا 20

كَلَّآ إِذَا دُكَّتِ ٱلۡأَرۡضُ دَكّٗا دَكّٗا 21

Read with Ghunnah — مْ ــًّ نْ مّ نّ
Read with Madd (stretch) — ــٓ ـِـيْ ـَا ـُو ـِي
Silent letters — ا و ي
Read with Qalqalah (echo) — د ج ب ط ق
Read with velerisation (Full Mouth) — خ ص ض غ ط ق ظ رُ

الفجر

وَّجَآءَ رَبُّكَ وَالْمَلَكُ صَفًّا صَفًّا (22) وَجِايْٓءَ

يَوْمَئِذٍۭ بِجَهَنَّمَ ج (STOP or CONTINUE) يَوْمَئِذٍ يَّتَذَكَّرُ الْاِنْسَانُ

وَاَنّٰى لَهُ الذِّكْرٰى (23) يَقُوْلُ يٰلَيْتَنِيْ

قَدَّمْتُ لِحَيَاتِيْ (24) فَيَوْمَئِذٍ لَّا يُعَذِّبُ

عَذَابَهٗٓ اَحَدٌ (25) وَّلَا يُوْثِقُ وَثَاقَهٗٓ اَحَدٌ (26)

يٰٓاَيَّتُهَا النَّفْسُ الْمُطْمَئِنَّةُ (27) ارْجِعِيْٓ اِلٰى

رَبِّكِ رَاضِيَةً مَّرْضِيَّةً (28) فَادْخُلِيْ فِيْ

عِبٰدِيْ (29) وَادْخُلِيْ جَنَّتِيْ (30) ع

ع 1 30 14

| | | |
|---|---|---|
| Excellent | Comments: | I need more help with: |
| Good | | Recognition |
| Repeat | | Articulation |
| | | Fluency |

Date Started: / /

Date Completed: / /

Read with Ghunnah: مْ نّ مّ نْ نّ

Read with Madd (stretch): ي و ا ء ~

Silent letters: ا و ي

Read with Qalqalah (echo): ق ط ب ج د

Read with velerisation (Full Mouth): ظ ط ض ص ق غ خ رُ

# The City

**Order in Mushaf:** 90

**Order in revelation:** 35



## About the Sūrah

Sūrah al-Balad gets its name from the word Al-Balad, meaning "The City" which appears in the first Āyah. The city referred to is Makkah, the sacred city, which Allāh ﷻ takes an oath upon, before describing some of the gifts and blessings He has given to humankind. These include our two eyes, which help us see right from wrong, our lips and tongue, which help us speak righteousness, and our intellect, which helps us to differentiate the right path from the wrong. Unfortunately, despite these favours, many people still fail to acknowledge Allāh's ﷻ bounty, thinking instead that they are self-sufficient and in control.

The Sūrah then discusses how following the right path is difficult, like climbing a hill, before describing some of the actions that allow us to be successful. These include: the freeing of slaves; feeding orphans, close relatives and the poor, and helping the needy. May Allāh ﷻ give us all the ability to carry out such actions and ascend the right path. Āmeen

## Al-Hadīth

Safiyyah bint Shaibah ﵂ narrates that Rasūlullāh ﷺ said:

"Verily Allāh ﷻ made this City sacred on the Day that He created the heavens and the Earth. Therefore it is sacred by the sanctity of Allāh ﷻ until the Day of Judgement. Its trees should not be uprooted and its bushes and grass should not be removed."

Source: Al-Bukhārī

سورة البلد

Ayah: 20

بِسۡمِ اللّٰهِ الرَّحۡمٰنِ الرَّحِيۡمِ

Ruku': 1

لَاۤ اُقۡسِمُ بِهٰذَا الۡبَلَدِ ﴿1﴾ وَاَنۡتَ حِلٌّۢ بِهٰذَا

الۡبَلَدِ ﴿2﴾ وَوَالِدٍ وَّمَا وَلَدَ ﴿3﴾ لَقَدۡ خَلَقۡنَا

الۡاِنۡسَانَ فِىۡ كَبَدٍ ﴿4﴾ اَيَحۡسَبُ اَنۡ لَّنۡ يَّقۡدِرَ

عَلَيۡهِ اَحَدٌ ﴿5﴾ يَقُوۡلُ اَهۡلَكۡتُ مَالًا لُّبَدًا ﴿6﴾

اَيَحۡسَبُ اَنۡ لَّمۡ يَرَهٗۤ اَحَدٌ ﴿7﴾ اَلَمۡ نَجۡعَلۡ

لَّهٗ عَيۡنَيۡنِ ﴿8﴾ وَلِسَانًا وَّشَفَتَيۡنِ ﴿9﴾ وَهَدَيۡنٰهُ

النَّجۡدَيۡنِ ﴿10﴾ فَلَا اقۡتَحَمَ الۡعَقَبَةَ ﴿11﴾

وَمَاۤ اَدۡرٰٮكَ مَا الۡعَقَبَةُ ﴿12﴾ فَكُّ رَقَبَةٍ ﴿13﴾

Read with Ghunnah: نّ مّ ن م
Read with Madd (stretch): ـٓ ا و ي
Silent letters: ا و ي
Read with Qalqalah (echo): ق ط ب ج د
Read with velerisation (Full Mouth): ظ ط ض ص ق غ خ ر

أَوْ إِطْعَٰمٌ فِى يَوْمٍ ذِى مَسْغَبَةٍ 14 يَتِيمًا

ذَا مَقْرَبَةٍ 15 أَوْ مِسْكِينًا ذَا مَتْرَبَةٍ 16

ثُمَّ كَانَ مِنَ ٱلَّذِينَ ءَامَنُوا۟ وَتَوَاصَوْا۟

بِٱلصَّبْرِ وَتَوَاصَوْا۟ بِٱلْمَرْحَمَةِ 17 أُو۟لَٰٓئِكَ

أَصْحَٰبُ ٱلْمَيْمَنَةِ 18 وَٱلَّذِينَ كَفَرُوا۟

بِـَٔايَٰتِنَا هُمْ أَصْحَٰبُ ٱلْمَشْـَٔمَةِ 19

ع عَلَيْهِمْ نَارٌ مُّؤْصَدَةٌۢ 20

ع 1 20 16

90 - The City

| Excellent | Comments: | I need more help with: | Date Started: / / |
| --- | --- | --- | --- |
| Good | | Recognition | Date Completed: / / |
| Repeat | | Articulation | |
| | | Fluency | |

Read with Ghunnah: مّ نّ ن ~ مْ
Read with Madd (stretch): ـــٓ ـٖ ـٰ و ي
Silent letters: ا و ي
Read with Qalqalah (echo): قْ طْ بْ جْ دْ
Read with velerisation (Full Mouth): خ ص ض غ ط ق ظ ر

# The Sun

Revealed in Makkah

**Order in Mushaf:** 91

**Order in revelation:** 26

## About the Sûrah

Sûrah ash-Shams gets its name from the word Ash-Shams, meaning "The Sun" which is used in the first Âyah.
The Sûrah begins by contrasting three pairs of opposites in Allâh's ﷻ creation: the sun and the moon, the night and the day and the heavens and the earth. These are used to highlight the differences between pure souls, which are free from disbelief, and their opposite, evil souls which are corrupted by disbelief.

The Sûrah also reminds us that Allâh ﷻ has given humans free will and the ability to choose between two opposing paths in life: the right and the wrong. And because we are free to choose our path, we are therefore also responsible for our choice. Thus, those who choose the path of righteousness will be successful in the eyes of Allâh ﷻ ,while those who choose the wrong path will be unsuccessful.

## Al-Hadîth

Ibn Abbâs narrates:

"Rasûlullâh ﷺ used to pause whenever he recited the eighth Âyah of Sûrah ash-Shams and recite the following prayer:

اللّٰهُمَّ اٰتِ نَفْسِيْ تَقْوَاهَا اَنْتَ وَلِيُّهَا وَمَوْلَاهَا وَخَيْرُ مَنْ زَكَّاهَا

"O Allâh! Give my soul its good.
You are its Guardian and Master, and the best to purify it."

Source: Imâm Tabarâni

سورة الشمس

Ruku': 1

# بِسۡمِ اللّٰهِ الرَّحۡمٰنِ الرَّحِيۡمِ

Āyah: 15

وَالشَّمۡسِ وَضُحٰهَا ﴿1﴾ وَالۡقَمَرِ اِذَا تَلٰهَا ﴿2﴾

وَالنَّهَارِ اِذَا جَلّٰهَا ﴿3﴾ وَالَّيۡلِ اِذَا يَغۡشٰهَا ﴿4﴾

وَالسَّمَآءِ وَمَا بَنٰهَا ﴿5﴾ وَالۡاَرۡضِ وَمَا طَحٰهَا

﴿6﴾ وَنَفۡسٍ وَّمَا سَوّٰهَا ﴿7﴾ فَاَلۡهَمَهَا فُجُوۡرَهَا

وَتَقۡوٰهَا ﴿8﴾ قَدۡ اَفۡلَحَ مَنۡ زَكّٰهَا ﴿9﴾

وَقَدۡ خَابَ مَنۡ دَسّٰهَا ﴿10﴾ كَذَّبَتۡ ثَمُوۡدُ

بِطَغۡوٰهَآ ﴿11﴾ اِذِ انۡۢبَعَثَ اَشۡقٰهَا ﴿12﴾ فَقَالَ

لَهُمۡ رَسُوۡلُ اللّٰهِ نَاقَةَ اللّٰهِ وَسُقۡيٰهَا ﴿13﴾

★ اَللّٰهُمَّ اٰتِ نَفۡسِيۡ تَقۡوٰهَا اَنۡتَ وَلِيُّهَا وَمَوۡلٰهَا وَخَيۡرُ مَنۡ زَكّٰهَا

91 - The Sun

Read with Ghunnah: مۡ ن ّ ن مّ نّ
Read with Madd (stretch): ي و ا ~
Silent letters: ا و ي
Read with Qalqalah (echo): د ج ب ط ق
Read with velerisation (Full Mouth): ظ ط ض ص ق غ خ ر

فَكَذَّبُوهُ فَعَقَرُوهَا فَدَمْدَمَ عَلَيْهِمْ رَبُّهُم
بِذَنۢبِهِمْ فَسَوَّىٰهَا 14 وَلَا يَخَافُ عُقْبَٰهَا 15

| Excellent | Comments: | I need more help with: | Date Started: / / |
|---|---|---|---|
| Good | | Recognition | Date Completed: / / |
| Repeat | | Articulation | |
| | | Fluency | |

Read with Ghunnah — Read with Madd (stretch) — Silent letters — Read with Qalqalah (echo) — Read with velerisation (Full Mouth)



مَا شَاءَ اللّٰه
You have just learnt another Sūrah from Al-Qur'ān

Don't forget to mark off on the progress sheet!

Jābir narrates: "Once a man was driving two camels and night had fallen. He found Mu'ādh [Mu'ādh ibn Jabal, a famous companion of The Prophet known as one of the best reciters of his time] performing [Īshā' prayers], so he made his camels kneel and joined Mu'ādh in the prayer. The latter recited Sūrah al-Baqarah or Sūrah an-Nisā' [both very long chapters from the Qur'ān], [so] the man left the prayer and went away [because he had been working all day, and was too tired to stand that long]. When [the man] came to know that Mu'ādh had criticized him [for leaving], he went to The Prophet, and complained against Mu'ādh The Prophet said three times, 'O Mu'ādh! Are you putting the people to trial? It would have been better if you had recited
Sabbi-his-ma rab-bi-kal 'a'lā (Sūrah al-'A'lā),
Wash-sham-si wa dū-hā-hā (Sūrah ash-Shams),
or Wal-lay-li idhā yagh-sha (Sūrah al-Layl),
for the old, the weak and the needy who pray behind you.' "
Source: Al-Bukhārī

# The Night

Revealed in Makkah

**Order in Mushaf:** 92

**Order in revelation:** 9

## About the Sûrah

Sûrah al-Layl gets its name from the word Al-Layl, meaning "The Night", which Allâh ﷻ takes an oath by in the first Âyah. The main topic of this Sûrah is how human beings can choose to act in different ways, and reminds us that if we choose to do good, Allâh ﷻ will make it easy for us to perform good acts, but warns us that if we choose the wrong path, Allâh ﷻ will make it easy for us to do wrong and thus fall further into wretchedness.

The Sûrah uses the differences between night and day and male and female to contrast the different choices people can make. It compares the pious to the impious; believers to unbelievers; the generous, who spend their wealth for Allâh's ﷻ sake, to the stingy and miserly; those who fear Allâh ﷻ to those who think they are self-sufficent and don't need him, and those who attest the truth to those who deny it. The Sûrah closes by mentioning a pious individual (usually believed to be the great companion Abu Bakr ؓ) who spends his wealth solely for Allâh's ﷻ sake.



## Al-Hadîth

**Abu Hurayrah ؓ narrates:**

"Rasûlullâh ﷺ said 'Whoever spends in the cause of AllWâh, the Mighty and Sublime, he will be hailed in Paradise: 'O slave of Alliâh, here is prosperity'. Whoever is one of the people of Salâh, he will be called from the gate of Salâh. Whoever is one of the people of charity, he will be called from the gate of Ar-Rayyan.' Abu Bakr As-Siddiq then said: 'O Rasûlullâh ﷺ ...Will there be anyone who will be called from all of these gates?' Rasûlullâh ﷺ replied: 'Yes, and I hope that you will be one of them.' "

**Source: An-Nasâî**

سورة الليل

Ruku': 1

بِسْمِ اللّٰهِ الرَّحْمٰنِ الرَّحِيْمِ

Āyah: 21

وَالَّيْلِ اِذَا يَغْشٰى (1) وَالنَّهَارِ اِذَا

تَجَلّٰى (2) وَمَا خَلَقَ الذَّكَرَ وَالْاُنْثٰٓى (3)

اِنَّ سَعْيَكُمْ لَشَتّٰى (4) فَاَمَّا مَنْ اَعْطٰى

وَاتَّقٰى (5) وَصَدَّقَ بِالْحُسْنٰى (6) فَسَنُيَسِّرُهٗ

لِلْيُسْرٰى (7) وَاَمَّا مَنْۢ بَخِلَ وَاسْتَغْنٰى (8)

وَكَذَّبَ بِالْحُسْنٰى (9) فَسَنُيَسِّرُهٗ لِلْعُسْرٰى (10)

وَمَا يُغْنِيْ عَنْهُ مَالُهٗٓ اِذَا تَرَدّٰى (11) اِنَّ عَلَيْنَا

لَلْهُدٰى (12) وَاِنَّ لَنَا لَلْاٰخِرَةَ وَالْاُوْلٰى (13)



Read with Ghunnah | Read with Madd (stretch) | Silent letters | Read with Qalqalah (echo) | Read with velerisation (Full Mouth)

فَأَنذَرْتُكُمْ نَارًا تَلَظَّىٰ 14 لَا يَصْلَاهَآ

إِلَّا ٱلْأَشْقَى 15 ٱلَّذِى كَذَّبَ وَتَوَلَّىٰ 16

وَسَيُجَنَّبُهَا ٱلْأَتْقَى 17 ٱلَّذِى يُؤْتِى

مَالَهُۥ يَتَزَكَّىٰ 18 وَمَا لِأَحَدٍ عِندَهُۥ

مِن نِّعْمَةٍ تُجْزَىٰٓ 19 إِلَّا ٱبْتِغَآءَ وَجْهِ

رَبِّهِ ٱلْأَعْلَىٰ 20 وَلَسَوْفَ يَرْضَىٰ 21 ع

92 - The Night

ع 1 21 17

Excellent ◯
Good ◯
Repeat ◯

Comments:

I need more help with:
Recognition ◯
Articulation ◯
Fluency ◯

Date Started: / /
Date Completed: / /

مْ نّ مّ ن ـً ـٍ ـٌ | يِ وُ ا ـٰ ـٓ | ا و ي | ق ط ب ج د | خ ص ض غ ط ق ظ رُ

Read with Ghunnah · Read with Madd (stretch) · Silent letters · Read with Qalqalah (echo) · Read with velerisation (Full Mouth)

مَا شَاءَ اللّٰه
You have just learnt another Sūrah from Al-Qur'ān

Don't forget to mark off on the progress sheet!

# The Morning Light

**Order in Mushaf:** **93**

**Order in revelation:** **11**

## About the Sûrah

Sûrah ad-Dhuhâ gets its name from the word Ad-Dhuhâ, meaning "The Bright Morning Light", which Allâh ﷻ takes an oath by in the first Âyah. Prior to this Sûrah being revealed, Rasulûllâh ﷺ had received no revelations for a long period of time, which had left him wondering if Allâh ﷻ had forsaken him, and led his opponents in Makkah to start taunting him. Finally, Allâh ﷻ revealed Sûrah ad-Dhuhâ, consoling Rasûlullâh ﷺ and assuring him that he had done nothing wrong.

The Sûrah reminds Rasûlullâh ﷺ that as an orphan, Allâh ﷻ had given him shelter; as one who was unaware, Allâh ﷻ had guided him and as one in need, Allâh ﷻ had provided for him. The Sûrah then goes on to command Rasûlullâh ﷺ, and us all, to be good to orphans, to never turn away those asking for help or seeking knowledge, and to declare the favours and blessings Allâh ﷻ has granted us by talking about them, as this is a way of showing gratitude to Him.

Sûrah ad-Dhuhâ is one of only three Sûrahs in the Qur'ân that speak directly to Rasûlullâh ﷺ about his special blessings and nothing else.

## Al-Hadîth

Jâbir رضي الله عنه narrates that Rasûlullâh ﷺ said:

**"Whoever is not thankful to the people is not thankful to Allâh"**

Source: At-Tirmidhî

الضحى

# سورة الضحى

Ruku': 1

بِسۡمِ اللّٰهِ الرَّحۡمٰنِ الرَّحِيۡمِ

Āyah: 11

وَالضُّحٰى ﴿1﴾ وَالَّيۡلِ اِذَا سَجٰى ﴿2﴾ مَا وَدَّعَكَ

رَبُّكَ وَمَا قَلٰى ﴿3﴾ وَلَلۡاٰخِرَةُ خَيۡرٌ لَّكَ مِنَ

الۡاُوۡلٰى ﴿4﴾ وَلَسَوۡفَ يُعۡطِيۡكَ رَبُّكَ فَتَرۡضٰى

﴿5﴾ اَلَمۡ يَجِدۡكَ يَتِيۡمًا فَاٰوٰى ﴿6﴾ وَوَجَدَكَ

ضَآلًّا فَهَدٰى ﴿7﴾ وَوَجَدَكَ عَآئِلًا فَاَغۡنٰى ﴿8﴾

فَاَمَّا الۡيَتِيۡمَ فَلَا تَقۡهَرۡ ﴿9﴾ وَاَمَّا السَّآئِلَ

فَلَا تَنۡهَرۡ ﴿10﴾ وَاَمَّا بِنِعۡمَةِ رَبِّكَ فَحَدِّثۡ ﴿11﴾ ع

1 11 18

93 - The Morning Light

Excellent

Good

Repeat

Comments:

I need more help with:

Recognition

Articulation

Fluency

Date Started: / /

Date Completed: / /

Read with Ghunnah

Read with Madd (stretch)

Silent letters

Read with Qalqalah (echo)

Read with velerisation (Full Mouth)

# Solace

**Order in Mushaf:** 94

**Order in revelation:** 21

## About the Sûrah

Sûrah ash-Sharh, also known as Sûrah al-Inshirâh, gets its name from the word nash-rah, meaning "Solace", used in the first Âyah. This Sûrah is very closely linked to the previous one (Sûrah ad-Dhuhâ), so much so that some of the Companions used to recite the two together during Salâh, with no break between.

Both Sûrahs mention the hardships that Rasûlullâh ﷺ was going through at that point in his Prophethood, and Sûrah ash-Sharh then goes on to console him by describing how his heart has been filled with light and wisdom, how he is free from sin and dirt and how his name has been exalted by being mentioned alongside Allâh's ﷻ e.g. in adhân, iqâmah, tashahhud and khutbah.

Finally, Allâh ﷻ gives us all solace by reminding us that after every hardship there will be ease, and repeats the words to reaffirm the point, before asking us to remember Him wholeheartedly.

## Al-Hadîth

Anas bin Mâlik رضي الله عنه narrates that Rasûlullâh ﷺ said:

"None of you has faith until I am more beloved to him than his children, his father, and all of the people."

Source: Al-Bukhârî

سورة الإنشراح

Ruku': 1 — بِسۡمِ اللّٰهِ الرَّحۡمٰنِ الرَّحِيۡمِ — Āyah: 8

اَلَمۡ نَشۡرَحۡ لَكَ صَدۡرَكَ ﴿1﴾ وَوَضَعۡنَا عَنۡكَ
وِزۡرَكَ ﴿2﴾ الَّذِىۡۤ اَنۡقَضَ ظَهۡرَكَ ﴿3﴾ وَرَفَعۡنَا
لَكَ ذِكۡرَكَ ﴿4﴾ فَاِنَّ مَعَ الۡعُسۡرِ يُسۡرًا ﴿5﴾
اِنَّ مَعَ الۡعُسۡرِ يُسۡرًا ﴿6﴾ فَاِذَا فَرَغۡتَ
فَانۡصَبۡ ﴿7﴾ وَاِلٰى رَبِّكَ فَارۡغَبۡ ﴿8﴾ ع

ع 1 8 19

| Excellent | Comments: | I need more help with: | Date Started: / / |
|---|---|---|---|
| Good | | Recognition | Date Completed: / / |
| Repeat | | Articulation | |
| | | Fluency | |

مّ نّ نۡ ںٓ مۡ — Read with Ghunnah
ـٰ ـٓ ا و ي — Read with Madd (stretch)
ا و ي — Silent letters
قۡ طۡ بۡ جۡ دۡ — Read with Qalqalah (echo)
رُ خ غ ق ص ض ط ظ — Read with velerisation (Full Mouth)

94 - Solace

مَا شَاءَ اللّٰه
You have just learnt another Sūrah from Al-Qur'ān

Don't forget to mark off on the progress sheet!

# The Fig

**Order in Mushaf:** 95

**Order in revelation:** 28

## About the Sûrah

Sûrah at-Teen gets its name from the word at-Teen, meaning "The Fig", which is found in the first Âyah. The Sûrah starts with Allâh ﷻ taking an oath on four items: i) the fig ii) the olive, iii) Mount Sinai iv) the City of Makkah. The terms used may be specific, or they could be metaphorical, referencing the lands of the Prophets wherein Allâh ﷻ revealed His Holy Books, the Tawrâh, the Injîl and the Qur'ân.

The main message of the Sûrah is that Allâh ﷻ has created human beings in a beautiful and honoured form, both physically and intellectually, but that due to our actions Allâh ﷻ can degrade us to being the lowest of the low. Allâh ﷻ then promises us that those who believe and do good will be saved from such a fate and receive reward without interruption.

## Al-Hadîth

Al-Barâ' bin 'Âzib رضي الله عنه narrates:

"Rasûlullâh ﷺ used to recite Surah At-Teen in one of his Raka'ah's while travelling, and I have never heard anyone with a nicer voice or recitation than him."

Source: Muslim

# سورة التين

Ruku': 1

بِسۡمِ اللّٰهِ الرَّحۡمٰنِ الرَّحِيۡمِ

Āyah: 8

وَالتِّيۡنِ وَالزَّيۡتُوۡنِ ۝1 وَطُوۡرِ سِيۡنِيۡنَ ۝2

وَهٰذَا الۡبَلَدِ الۡاَمِيۡنِ ۝3 لَقَدۡ خَلَقۡنَا

الۡاِنۡسَانَ فِىۡۤ اَحۡسَنِ تَقۡوِيۡمٍ ۝4 ثُمَّ

رَدَدۡنٰهُ اَسۡفَلَ سٰفِلِيۡنَ ۝5 اِلَّا الَّذِيۡنَ

اٰمَنُوۡا وَعَمِلُوا الصّٰلِحٰتِ فَلَهُمۡ اَجۡرٌ غَيۡرُ

مَمۡنُوۡنٍ ۝6 فَمَا يُكَذِّبُكَ بَعۡدُ بِالدِّيۡنِ ۝7

اَلَيۡسَ اللّٰهُ بِاَحۡكَمِ الۡحٰكِمِيۡنَ ۝8 ع

ع 1 8 20

بَلٰى وَاَنَا عَلٰى ذٰلِكَ مِنَ الشّٰهِدِيۡنَ

| Excellent | Good | Repeat |
|---|---|---|
| | | |

Comments:

I need more help with:
- Recognition
- Articulation
- Fluency

Date Started: / /

Date Completed: / /

Read with Ghunnah: مّ ـًـٍـ نۡ مّ نّ

Read with Madd (stretch): ـٓ ـٰ ـُـو ـِـي

Silent letters: ا و ي

Read with Qalqalah (echo): قۡ طۡ بۡ جۡ دۡ

Read with velerisation (Full Mouth): ظ ط ض ص ق غ خ رُ

# The Clot

**Order in Mushaf:** 96

**Order in revelation:** 1

## About the Sûrah

Sûrah al-'Alaq is named after the word **'Alaq**, meaning a "clot of blood" which is mentioned in the first Âyah. The first five verses of the Sûrah are famous for being the very first words of the Qur'ân revealed by Allâh ﷻ to our beloved Prophet ﷺ through the Angel Jibra'eel عليه السلام. The verses exhort us to 'read' or 'recite' in the name of Allâh ﷻ, who created human beings from the merest clot of blood (or cell) and thereafter taught us to use the pen (to write and transmit information), and gave us knowledge which we did not previously have.

These first five verses were revealed to Rasûlullâh ﷺ during Ramadhân in the year 610 CE, while he was meditating in the cave of Hirâ on Mount an-Nûr. The rest of the Sûrah was revealed after a period known as the 'Fatrah' which lasted several years. These latter verses command us to turn to Allâh ﷻ and not transgress. It warns those who reject him and ends with a command to perform Sajdah (prostration), which we should all do after reading the final verse.

## Al-Hadîth

**Ubâdah ibn As-Sâmit رضي الله عنه narrates that Rasûlullâh ﷺ said:**

"The first thing Allâh created was the pen. He told it to write, so it wrote what was to take place until the end of time. This is with Allâh on His throne."

Source: At-Tirmidhî

سورة العلق

Ruku': 1

# بِسۡمِ اللّٰهِ الرَّحۡمٰنِ الرَّحِيۡمِ

Āyah: 19

اِقۡرَاۡ بِاسۡمِ رَبِّكَ الَّذِىۡ خَلَقَ ۝1

خَلَقَ الۡاِنۡسَانَ مِنۡ عَلَقٍ ۝2 اِقۡرَاۡ وَرَبُّكَ

الۡاَكۡرَمُ ۝3 الَّذِىۡ عَلَّمَ بِالۡقَلَمِ ۝4

عَلَّمَ الۡاِنۡسَانَ مَا لَمۡ يَعۡلَمۡ ۝5 كَلَّاۤ اِنَّ

الۡاِنۡسَانَ لَيَطۡغٰٓى ۝6 اَنۡ رَّاٰهُ اسۡتَغۡنٰى ۝7

اِنَّ اِلٰى رَبِّكَ الرُّجۡعٰى ۝8 اَرَءَيۡتَ الَّذِىۡ

يَنۡهٰى ۝9 عَبۡدًا اِذَا صَلّٰى ۝10 اَرَءَيۡتَ اِنۡ

كَانَ عَلَى الۡهُدٰٓى ۝11 اَوۡ اَمَرَ بِالتَّقۡوٰى ۝12

Read with Ghunnah | Read with Madd (stretch) | Silent letters | Read with Qalqalah (echo) | Read with velerisation (Full Mouth)

العلق

أَرَءَيْتَ إِن كَذَّبَ وَتَوَلَّىٰ (13) أَلَمْ يَعْلَم

بِأَنَّ ٱللَّهَ يَرَىٰ (14) كَلَّا لَئِن لَّمْ يَنتَهِ

لَنَسْفَعًۢا بِٱلنَّاصِيَةِ (15) نَاصِيَةٍ كَٰذِبَةٍ خَاطِئَةٍ

(16) فَلْيَدْعُ نَادِيَهُۥ (17) سَنَدْعُ ٱلزَّبَانِيَةَ

(18) كَلَّا لَا تُطِعْهُ وَٱسْجُدْ وَٱقْتَرِب ۩ Perform a Prostration (19) السجدة ع

ع 1 19 21

السجدة Prostration

Excellent | Good | Repeat

Comments:

I need more help with: Recognition | Articulation | Fluency

Date Started: / /

Date Completed: / /

Read with Ghunnah | Read with Madd (stretch) | Silent letters | Read with Qalqalah (echo) | Read with velerisation (Full Mouth)

## (Optional) Du'â when making Sajdah at-Tilâwah (prostrating)

اَللّٰهُمَّ لَكَ سَجَدْتُّ وَبِكَ اٰمَنْتُ ، وَلَكَ اَسْلَمْتُ،

O Allâh, unto You I have prostrated and in You I have believed, and unto You I have submitted.

سَجَدَ وَجْهِيَ لِلَّذِىْ خَلَقَهٗ وَصَوَّرَهٗ وَشَقَّ سَمْعَهٗ وَبَصَرَهٗ،

My face has prostrated before He Who created it and fashioned it, and brought forth its faculties of hearing and seeing.

بِحَوْلِهٖ وَقُوَّتِهٖ تَبَارَكَ اللّٰهُ اَحْسَنُ الْخَالِقِيْنَ

Blessed is Allâh, the best of creators.

Sources: Muslim, Abu-Dâ'wûd, At-Tirmidhî, An-Nasâ'î and Ibn Mâjah

# The Power

Order in Mushaf: **97**

Order in revelation: **25**

## About the Sūrah

Sūrah al-Qadr gets its name from the word Qadr, found in the first Âyah, which means 'majesty' or 'power', but can also mean 'decree' or 'destiny'. The Sūrah talks about the qualities of the 'Night of Power' (Laylatul Qadr), the most blessed night in the month of Ramadhān. The Night of Power was when the Qur'ān was sent down by Allāh from al-Lawh al-Mahfūdh (The Preserved Tablet) to Baytul-'Izzah (The House of Might) in the earthly heavens. Thereafter it was sent down to Rasūlullāh ﷺ in parts over many years, with the very first verses being revealed on this night in the year 610 CE.

The Sūrah tells us that the Night of Power is better than a thousand months (meaning a vast amount of time), that Jibra'eel عليه السلام and other Angels descend into the world on this night, and that peace reigns until the coming of the dawn.

The exact date of The Night of Power is not known, thus encouraging us to carry out worship and good deeds as often as possible in order to be sure of finding it.

## Al-Hadīth

Abu Hurayrah رضي الله عنه narrates that Rasūlullāh ﷺ said:

"Whoever stands in prayer (i.e carries out any form of worship) during the Night of al-Qadr, with full faith and expectation of reward from Allāh, his previous sins will be forgiven"

Source: Al-Bukhārī

سورة القدر

Ruku': 1 بِسۡمِ اللّٰهِ الرَّحۡمٰنِ الرَّحِيۡمِ Āyah: 5

اِنَّاۤ اَنۡزَلۡنٰهُ فِىۡ لَيۡلَةِ الۡقَدۡرِ ۚ (1) وَمَاۤ اَدۡرٰٮكَ

مَا لَيۡلَةُ الۡقَدۡرِ ؕ (2) لَيۡلَةُ الۡقَدۡرِ ۙ خَيۡرٌ مِّنۡ

اَلۡفِ شَهۡرٍ ؕ (3) تَنَزَّلُ الۡمَلٰٓئِكَةُ وَالرُّوۡحُ

فِيۡهَا بِاِذۡنِ رَبِّهِمۡ‌ۚ مِّنۡ كُلِّ اَمۡرٍ ۛۙ (4)

سَلٰمٌ ۛ هِىَ حَتّٰى مَطۡلَعِ الۡفَجۡرِ (5) ع

ع 10 2 2

الثلثة Three-Quarters of the Juz

القدر

Excellent
Good
Repeat

Comments:

I need more help with:
Recognition
Articulation
Fluency

Date Started: / /
Date Completed: / /

Read with Ghunnah — Read with Madd (stretch) — Silent letters — Read with Qalqalah (echo) — Read with velerisation (Full Mouth)

مَا شَاءَ اللّٰه
You have just learnt another Sūrah from Al-Qur'ān

Don't forget to mark off on the progress sheet!

# The Clear Proof

**Order in Mushaf:** 98

**Order in revelation:** 100

## About the Sûrah

Sûrah al-Bayyinah gets its name from the word **Bayyinah**, meaning "Clear Proof" which Allâh ﷻ mentions in the first Âyah.
This Sûrah discusses the role of the Qur'ân and Rasûlullâh ﷺ in delivering Allâh's ﷻ Message to humankind. In particular it talks about the People of the Book, who were given Divine Revelations in the past but who then deviated from their original scriptures. The Sûrah says that one reason Rasûlullâh ﷺ was sent the Qur'ân was to correct those deviations by presenting the pure, uncorrupted Message once again. For the People of the Book, The Qur'ân contains the same Message they had already received in the past, making it difficult for them to deny its divinity (although many still did). The Qur'ân has also been sent as a guidance to those who have not received prior scriptures; it is a clear Message for all humankind and applies until the end of time.
The Sûrah reiterates the key Message of Islam, which is to worship only Allâh ﷻ and associate no partners with Him, and reminds us, finally, that those who do good and believe in Allâh ﷻ will gain the best of rewards.



## Al-Hadîth

'Abdullâh bin 'Amr رضي الله عنه narrates that Rasûlullâh ﷺ said:

"Fasting and the Qur'ân will intercede for the slave on the Day of Judgement. Fasting will say, 'O My Lord! I prevented him from food and desires, so accept my intercession for him.' And the Qur'ân will say, 'I prevented him from sleep during the night, so accept my intercession for him.'...thus they will intercede."

Source: Musnad of Imâm Ahmad

سورة البينة

Ruku': 1

بِسۡمِ اللّٰهِ الرَّحۡمٰنِ الرَّحِيۡمِ

Āyah: 8

لَمۡ يَكُنِ الَّذِيۡنَ كَفَرُوۡا مِنۡ اَهۡلِ الۡكِتٰبِ

وَالۡمُشۡرِكِيۡنَ مُنۡفَكِّيۡنَ حَتّٰى تَاۡتِيَهُمُ الۡبَيِّنَةُ

1 رَسُوۡلٌ مِّنَ اللّٰهِ يَتۡلُوۡا صُحُفًا مُّطَهَّرَةً 2

فِيۡهَا كُتُبٌ قَيِّمَةٌ 3 وَمَا تَفَرَّقَ الَّذِيۡنَ

اُوۡتُوا الۡكِتٰبَ اِلَّا مِنۡۢ بَعۡدِ مَا جَآءَتۡهُمُ

الۡبَيِّنَةُ 4 وَمَاۤ اُمِرُوۡۤا اِلَّا لِيَعۡبُدُوا اللّٰهَ

مُخۡلِصِيۡنَ لَهُ الدِّيۡنَ حُنَفَآءَ وَيُقِيۡمُوا الصَّلٰوةَ

وَيُؤۡتُوا الزَّكٰوةَ ج STOP or CONTINUE وَذٰلِكَ دِيۡنُ الۡقَيِّمَةِ 5

Read with Ghunnah | Read with Madd (stretch) | Silent letters | Read with Qalqalah (echo) | Read with velerisation (Full Mouth)

إِنَّ الَّذِينَ كَفَرُوا مِنْ أَهْلِ الْكِتٰبِ

وَالْمُشْرِكِينَ فِي نَارِ جَهَنَّمَ خٰلِدِينَ

فِيهَا ج (STOP or CONTINUE) أُولٰٓئِكَ هُمْ شَرُّ الْبَرِيَّةِ ﴿6﴾ إِنَّ

الَّذِينَ ءَامَنُوا وَعَمِلُوا الصّٰلِحٰتِ أُولٰٓئِكَ

هُمْ خَيْرُ الْبَرِيَّةِ ﴿7﴾ جَزَآؤُهُمْ عِنْدَ رَبِّهِمْ

جَنّٰتُ عَدْنٍ تَجْرِي مِنْ تَحْتِهَا الْأَنْهٰرُ

خٰلِدِينَ فِيهَآ أَبَدًا صلى (BETTER to CONTINUE) رَّضِيَ اللّٰهُ عَنْهُمْ

2 ع 8 23 وَرَضُوا عَنْهُ ج (STOP or CONTINUE) ذٰلِكَ لِمَنْ خَشِيَ رَبَّهُ ﴿8﴾



Excellent | Good | Repeat

Comments:

I need more help with: Recognition / Articulation / Fluency

Date Started: / /

Date Completed: / /

Read with Ghunnah | Read with Madd (stretch) | Silent letters | Read with Qalqalah (echo) | Read with velerisation (Full Mouth)

# The Earthquake

Revealed in Makkah

Order in Mushaf: **99**

Order in revelation: **93**

## About the Sûrah

Sûrah al-Zalzalah, also known as al-Zilzâl gets its name from the word Zalzâlahâ, which means 'Earthquake' and which Allâh ﷻ mentions in the first Âyah.

The Sûrah concentrates on the demise of the world and the great earthquake which will usher in The Day of Judgement. It describes how people will be overawed by the force of the upheaval and destruction, and how the earth will bring forth all that is hidden within it, including evidence of mankind's actions. Indeed, Allâh ﷻ will inspire the earth itself to bear witness to all our deeds, so that no act, however small, will remain hidden.

It's easy for us to forget most of the things we have done in our lives, good or bad, but this Sûrah reminds us that on the Day of Judgement each and every action, however small or forgotten, will be examined and we will see every atom's weight of good and every atom's weight of evil we have done in our lives.

## Al-Hadîth

Abu Hurayrah ؓ narrates that Rasûlullâh ﷺ said:

"The Hour [Last Day] will not be established until [religious] knowledge is taken away [due to the death of religious scholars], earthquakes become very frequent, time begins to pass more quickly, many types of afflictions start to appear, murder increases and money starts to overflow amongst you."

Source: Al-Bukhârî

سورة الزلزلة

Āyah: 8 | Ruku': 1

بِسۡمِ اللّٰهِ الرَّحۡمٰنِ الرَّحِيۡمِ

اِذَا زُلۡزِلَتِ الۡاَرۡضُ زِلۡزَالَهَا ﴿1﴾ وَاَخۡرَجَتِ

الۡاَرۡضُ اَثۡقَالَهَا ﴿2﴾ وَقَالَ الۡاِنۡسَانُ

مَا لَهَا ﴿3﴾ يَوۡمَئِذٍ تُحَدِّثُ اَخۡبَارَهَا ﴿4﴾

بِاَنَّ رَبَّكَ اَوۡحٰى لَهَا ﴿5﴾ يَوۡمَئِذٍ يَّصۡدُرُ

النَّاسُ اَشۡتَاتًا لِّيُرَوۡا اَعۡمَالَهُمۡ ﴿6﴾

فَمَنۡ يَّعۡمَلۡ مِثۡقَالَ ذَرَّةٍ خَيۡرًا يَّرَهٗ ﴿7﴾

وَمَنۡ يَّعۡمَلۡ مِثۡقَالَ ذَرَّةٍ شَرًّا يَّرَهٗ ﴿8﴾ ع

ع 1 8 24

99 - The Earthquake

Excellent
Good
Repeat

Comments:

I need more help with:
Recognition
Articulation
Fluency

Date Started: / /
Date Completed: / /

| Read with Ghunnah | Read with Madd (stretch) | Silent letters | Read with Qalqalah (echo) | Read with velerisation (Full Mouth) |
|---|---|---|---|---|
| مّ نّ نْ ـً ـٍ ـٌ مْ | ~ ـٓ ـٰ ا و ي | ا و ي | ق ط ب ج د | خ غ ق ص ض ط ظ رُ |

# The Running Horses

Revealed in Makkah

**Order in Mushaf:** 100

**Order in revelation:** 14

## About the Sûrah

Sûrah al-'Âdiyât gets its name from the word **'Âdiyât**, meaning 'Running Horses' or 'War Horses', which Allâh ﷻ mentions in the first Âyah.

This Sûrah is about the ingratitude of human beings. It begins with a series of oaths taken on the gallant behaviour of horses during battle; how they are so loyal to their masters that they will risk their lives and go into the heat of battle willingly. This is then compared to human beings who are given far more favours by our Lord, but remain disloyal and ungrateful to Him.

The Sûrah explains how we are witnesses to our own ingratitude; we know we are being disloyal to the One who gives us everything, but our love of the world, and of wealth, means we remain hard-hearted. And it reminds us that when we are raised on the Day of Judgement, everything that is in our hearts will be made clear, and that Allâh ﷻ is well aware of everything in our hearts and everything we do.

## Al-Hadîth

'Abdullâh bin 'Amr رضي الله عنه narrates:

"It was said to Rasûlullâh ﷺ: 'Which of the people is best?' He replied: 'Everyone who is pure of heart and sincere in speech'. They said: 'Sincere in speech; we know what that is, but what does pure of heart mean?' He replied: 'It means [the heart] that is pious and pure, with no sin, injustice, rancour or envy in it.' "

Source: Ibn Mâjah

العاديات

سورة العاديات

Ayah: 11 | Ruku': 1

بِسۡمِ اللّٰهِ الرَّحۡمٰنِ الرَّحِيۡمِ

وَالۡعٰدِيٰتِ ضَبۡحًا ﴿1﴾ فَالۡمُوۡرِيٰتِ قَدۡحًا

﴿2﴾ فَالۡمُغِيۡرٰتِ صُبۡحًا ﴿3﴾ فَاَثَرۡنَ بِهٖ نَقۡعًا

﴿4﴾ فَوَسَطۡنَ بِهٖ جَمۡعًا ﴿5﴾ اِنَّ الۡاِنۡسَانَ لِرَبِّهٖ

لَكَنُوۡدٌ ﴿6﴾ وَاِنَّهٗ عَلٰى ذٰلِكَ لَشَهِيۡدٌ ﴿7﴾ وَاِنَّهٗ

لِحُبِّ الۡخَيۡرِ لَشَدِيۡدٌ ﴿8﴾ اَفَلَا يَعۡلَمُ اِذَا بُعۡثِرَ

مَا فِى الۡقُبُوۡرِ ﴿9﴾ وَحُصِّلَ مَا فِى الصُّدُوۡرِ

﴿10﴾ اِنَّ رَبَّهُمۡ بِهِمۡ يَوۡمَئِذٍ لَّخَبِيۡرٌ ﴿11﴾ ع

ع 1 11 25

100 - The Running Horses

Excellent | Good | Repeat

Comments:

I need more help with: Recognition / Articulation / Fluency

Date Started: / /

Date Completed: / /

Read with Ghunnah: مْ ـنّ نْ مّ نّ

Read with Madd (stretch): يِ ُو ـَا ءٍ ~

Silent letters: ا و ي

Read with Qalqalah (echo): قْ طْ بْ جْ دْ

Read with velerisation (Full Mouth): ظ ط ض ص ق غ خ رُ

# The Calamity

Order in Mushaf: **101**

Order in revelation: **30**

## About the Sûrah

Sûrah al-Qâri'ah gets its name from the word Al-Qâri'ah, which is found in the first Âyah, and which means "the calamity" or "the catastrophe".

Al-Qâri'ah is one of the many names for the Day of Judgement found in the Qur'ân and this Sûrah aims to impress upon mankind just what that Day will entail. It begins by asking us whether we know what 'The Calamity' really means, before telling us that on that day human beings will be bewildered and lost like moths scattered far and wide, and even the biggest and heaviest mountains will be dispersed like fluffs of wool.

The Sûrah also reminds us that on that Day our deeds will be weighed and those whose balances are heavy on the side of good deeds will enter a life of bliss, while those whose good deeds are outweighed by their bad will enter the abyss.

## Al-Hadîth

'Aa'îshah ﷺ narrates that Rasûlullâh ﷺ said:

"Do good deeds properly, sincerely and moderately, and know that your deeds [alone] will not enter you into Paradise [rather Allâh's mercy will], and the most beloved deed to Allâh is one that is regular and constant, even if it is little."

Source: Al-Bukhârî

سورة القارعة

Ruku': 1

بِسۡمِ اللّٰهِ الرَّحۡمٰنِ الرَّحِيۡمِ

Āyah: 11

اَلۡقَارِعَةُ ۝1 مَا الۡقَارِعَةُ ۝2 وَمَاۤ اَدۡرٰىكَ

مَا الۡقَارِعَةُ ۝3 يَوۡمَ يَكُوۡنُ النَّاسُ

كَالۡفَرَاشِ الۡمَبۡثُوۡثِ ۝4 وَتَكُوۡنُ الۡجِبَالُ

كَالۡعِهۡنِ الۡمَنۡفُوۡشِ ۝5 فَاَمَّا مَنۡ ثَقُلَتۡ

مَوَازِيۡنُهٗ ۝6 فَهُوَ فِيۡ عِيۡشَةٍ رَّاضِيَةٍ ۝7

وَاَمَّا مَنۡ خَفَّتۡ مَوَازِيۡنُهٗ ۝8 فَاُمُّهٗ هَاوِيَةٌ

وَمَاۤ اَدۡرٰىكَ مَا هِيَهۡ ۝9 نَارٌ حَامِيَةٌ ۝10 ع ۝11

ع 1 11 26

Excellent

Good

Repeat

Comments:

I need more help with:

Recognition

Articulation

Fluency

Date Started: / /

Date Completed: / /

Read with Ghunnah

Read with Madd (stretch)

Silent letters

Read with Qalqalah (echo)

Read with velerisation (Full Mouth)

# The Rivalry

**Order in Mushaf:** 102

**Order in revelation:** 16

## About the Sûrah

Sûrah at-Takâthur gets its name from the word At-Takâthur, found in the first Âyah, which means "accumulation" or "abundance", in this case regarding the pursuit of wealth.

Thus the subject of this Sûrah is mankind's tendency to pursue worldly riches and accumulate ever-increasing riches, even to the point of competing with each other to become the wealthiest and most powerful. The Sûrah tells us that worldly riches are of no benefit in the next life (âkhirah) and reminds us that constantly pursuing and increasing wealth will leave us little time to complete our spiritual duties towards Allâh ﷻ or increase our worship and good deeds.

Those who are obsessed by wealth and neglect their spiritual obligations will realise with certainty in the next life that their worldly goods have been left behind in this world and that none of them will be of any use at all, whereas those who have carried out worship and good deeds in abundance will find them waiting in the hereafter.

## Al-Hadîth

Anas bin Mâlik رضي الله عنه narrates that Rasûlullâh ﷺ said:

"Three things follow a deceased person [to the grave] and two of them return while one remains. The three things are: their family, their wealth and their deeds. Their family and their wealth return, while their deeds remain."

Source: Al-Bukhârî

# سورة التكاثر

Ruku': 1

بِسْمِ اللَّهِ الرَّحْمَٰنِ الرَّحِيمِ

Āyah: 8

أَلْهَىٰكُمُ التَّكَاثُرُ (1) حَتَّىٰ زُرْتُمُ الْمَقَابِرَ

(2) كَلَّا سَوْفَ تَعْلَمُونَ (3) ثُمَّ كَلَّا سَوْفَ

تَعْلَمُونَ (4) كَلَّا لَوْ تَعْلَمُونَ عِلْمَ الْيَقِينِ

(5) لَتَرَوُنَّ الْجَحِيمَ (6) ثُمَّ لَتَرَوُنَّهَا عَيْنَ

الْيَقِينِ (7) ثُمَّ لَتُسْأَلُنَّ يَوْمَئِذٍ عَنِ النَّعِيمِ (8) ع

ع 1 8 27



Excellent | Good | Repeat

Comments:

I need more help with: Recognition / Articulation / Fluency

Date Started: / /

Date Completed: / /

Read with Ghunnah | Read with Madd (stretch) | Silent letters | Read with Qalqalah (echo) | Read with velerisation (Full Mouth)

**Allāh, Most High, says in the Qur'ān:**

**"Then do they not reflect upon the Qur'ān? If it had been from [any] other than Allāh, they would have found within it much contradiction."**

**[Al-Qur'ān: 4:82]**

# Time

Revealed in Makkah

Order in Mushaf: **103**

Order in revelation: **13**

## About the Sûrah

Sûrah al-'Asr gets its name from the word Al-'Asr, which is found in the first Âyah. The word can mean "time" but can also mean "the declining day" or "eventide" (as in the evening prayer Salâtul-'Asr). All three meanings are fitting because the Sûrah focusses on the importance, and fleeting nature, of time and how short our lives are. And to further emphasise how short our time in the world is, Sûrah al-'Asr is the third shortest chapter in the whole Qur'ân.

In its three short verses, Sûrah al-'Asr reminds us that due to the shortness of life, human beings are always in a state of loss. Our time is quickly passing us by, literally second by second, and the only people who are gaining are those who spend that time doing good deeds, and encouraging others towards truth and patience.

## Al-Hadîth

'Abdullâh bin 'Abbâs narrates that Rasûlullâh said:

"There are two blessings which many people lose:

[They are] health and free time for doing good."

Source: Al-Bukhârî

سورة العصر

Ruku': 1

بِسْمِ اللّٰهِ الرَّحْمٰنِ الرَّحِيْمِ

Āyah: 3

وَالْعَصْرِ ﴿1﴾ اِنَّ الْاِنْسَانَ لَفِيْ خُسْرٍ ﴿2﴾

اِلَّا الَّذِيْنَ اٰمَنُوْا وَعَمِلُوا الصّٰلِحٰتِ

وَتَوَاصَوْا بِالْحَقِّ وَتَوَاصَوْا بِالصَّبْرِ ﴿3﴾ ع



1 ع 3 28

| Excellent | Comments: | I need more help with: | Date Started: / / |
|---|---|---|---|
| Good | | Recognition | Date Completed: / / |
| Repeat | | Articulation | |
| | | Fluency | |

Read with Ghunnah | Read with Madd (stretch) | Silent letters | Read with Qalqalah (echo) | Read with velerisation (Full Mouth)

مَا شَاءَ اللّٰه
You have just learnt another Sûrah from Al-Qur'ān

Don't forget to mark off on the progress sheet!

**Abu Hurayrah narrates that Rasûlullāh said:**
**"Learn the Qur'ān and recite it, because the example of one who learns the Qur'ān, reads it and recites it in Tahajjud is like an open bag full of musk; the fragrance spreads over the entire place. But a person who has learnt the Qur'ān and sleeps while the Qur'ān is in his heart, is like a bag full of musk but with its mouth closed."**
**Source: At-Tirmidhī**

# The Slanderer

**Order in Mushaf:** 104

**Order in revelation:** 32

## About the Sûrah

Sûrah al-Humazah gets its name from the word al-Humazah, which means "The Slanderer" and which is found in the first Âyah. The Sûrah warns against three very bad qualities commonly found among humans:

i) the tendency to slander and make fun of people and talk about them behind their backs (i.e to defame people using speech)
ii) the tendency to find fault in, or attack the character or honour of, others via writing or non-verbal actions (such as making faces)
iii) the tendency to be miserly; to hoard wealth and enjoy pouring over it (and even boast about it), rather than spend it on good causes, or to help others or even just to help oneself

The above three bad traits are greatly disliked by Allâh ﷻ and Sûrah al-Humazah warns us very severely against them. In particular, the Sûrah mentions how the hoarders think that their wealth will protect them and help them live forever, when the reality is very different; only Allâh ﷻ can protect us from difficulties.

## Al-Hadîth

Abu Hurayrah ؓ narrates that Rasûlullâh ﷺ said:

"Charity does not in any way decrease the wealth, and the one who forgives, Allâh adds to his respect, and the one who shows humility, Allâh elevates him in the estimation [of the people]."

Source: Muslim

سورة الهمزة

Ruku': 1

بِسۡمِ اللّٰهِ الرَّحۡمٰنِ الرَّحِيۡمِ

Âyah: 9

وَيۡلٌ لِّكُلِّ هُمَزَةٍ لُّمَزَةِ ۨ ﴿1﴾ الَّذِىۡ جَمَعَ

مَالًا وَّعَدَّدَهٗ ﴿2﴾ يَحۡسَبُ اَنَّ مَالَهٗۤ

اَخۡلَدَهٗ ﴿3﴾ كَلَّا ‌ لَيُنۡۢبَذَنَّ فِى الۡحُطَمَةِ ﴿4﴾

BETTER to CONTINUE (صلے)

وَمَاۤ اَدۡرٰٮكَ مَا الۡحُطَمَةُ ﴿5﴾ نَارُ اللّٰهِ

الۡمُوۡقَدَةُ ﴿6﴾ الَّتِىۡ تَطَّلِعُ عَلَى

الۡاَفۡـِٕدَةِ ﴿7﴾ اِنَّهَا عَلَيۡهِمۡ مُّؤۡصَدَةٌ ﴿8﴾

فِىۡ عَمَدٍ مُّمَدَّدَةٍ ﴿9﴾ ع

1 ع 9 29

104 - The Slanderer

Excellent
Good
Repeat

Comments:

I need more help with:
Recognition
Articulation
Fluency

Date Started: / /

Date Completed: / /

Read with Ghunnah | Read with Madd (stretch) | Silent letters | Read with Qalqalah (echo) | Read with velerisation (Full Mouth)

# The Elephant

Revealed in Makkah

**Order in Mushaf:** 105

**Order in revelation:** 19

## About the Sûrah

Sûrah al-Fîl gets its name from the word **Fîl** which means "Elephant" and which is mentioned in the first Âyah.

The Sûrah talks about an event that took place about forty years prior to the birth of Rasûlullâh ﷺ. King Abrahah of Yemen wanted to destroy the Ka'bah, so that he could stop the Hajj taking place there (he wanted to organise an alternative gathering in Yemen because of the wealth, power and status it would bring him). So he sent an army accompanied by huge African elephants to attack the Ka'bah. The Makkans of the time were terrified and ran to the mountains to hide, but Allâh ﷻ had a plan to thwart the attack. He sent successive flocks of small birds each carrying three stones which were cast upon the army with huge force, defeating it and saving the Ka'bah. Thus by Allâh's ﷻ will, the smallest of birds were able to defeat the biggest of elephants and a whole army of soldiers as well.

الفيل

## Al-Hadîth

Ibn 'Abbâs ؓ narrates that Maimoonah the wife of Rasûlullâh ﷺ said:

"Whoever prays in the Masjid of the Messenger of Allâh ﷺ [is doing good], for I heard the Messenger of Allâh ﷺ say: 'One prayer offered there is better than a thousand prayers offered elsewhere, except the Masjid of the Ka'bah.' "

Source: An-Nasâ'î

سورة الفيل

Ruku': 1

بِسۡمِ اللّٰهِ الرَّحۡمٰنِ الرَّحِيۡمِ

Āyah: 5

اَلَمۡ تَرَ كَيۡفَ فَعَلَ رَبُّكَ بِاَصۡحٰبِ

الۡفِيۡلِ ﴿1﴾ اَلَمۡ يَجۡعَلۡ كَيۡدَهُمۡ فِىۡ

تَضۡلِيۡلٍ ﴿2﴾ وَّاَرۡسَلَ عَلَيۡهِمۡ طَيۡرًا

اَبَابِيۡلَ ﴿3﴾ تَرۡمِيۡهِمۡ بِحِجَارَةٍ مِّنۡ

سِجِّيۡلٍ ﴿4﴾ فَجَعَلَهُمۡ كَعَصۡفٍ مَّاۡكُوۡلٍ ﴿5﴾ ع

ع 1 5 30

105 - The Elephant

Excellent
Good
Repeat

Comments:

I need more help with:
Recognition
Articulation
Fluency

Date Started: / /

Date Completed: / /

Read with Ghunnah | Read with Madd (stretch) | Silent letters | Read with Qalqalah (echo) | Read with velerisation (Full Mouth)

مَا شَاءَ اللّٰه
You have just learnt another Sūrah from Al-Qur'ān

Don't forget to mark off on the progress sheet!

# The Quraish

Revealed in Makkah

Order in Mushaf: **106**

Order in revelation: **29**

## About the Sûrah

Sûrah Quraish gets its name from the word **Quraish**, which is found in the first Âyah. "Quraish" is the name of a famous and pre-eminent Arab tribe, which was based in Makkah and which Rasûlullâh ﷺ belonged to. This Sûrah is linked with, and carries a similar message to, Sûrah al-Fîl, which precedes it, reminding the people of Quraish about the favours and bounties Allâh has bestowed upon them. In particular, the Sûrah talks about the protection that Allâh ﷻ had granted the tribe, during their travels and trade journeys, in summer and in winter, and while at home, and the freedom from hunger and security from fear they enjoyed.

As the Quraish were famous and respected, because they were seen as the caretakers of the Ka'bah, the holy site which people from all over Arabia would travel to for pilgrimage every year, Sûrah al-Quraish urges them to worship Allâh ﷻ, the Lord of the very same Ka'bah which earned them that fame and respect.

## Al-Hadîth

**Wathîlah bin Al-Asqâ ؓ narrates that Rasûlullâh ﷺ said:**

"Indeed, Allâh chose Kinanah from the children of Ismâ'îl, and He chose Quraish from Kinanah, and He chose Hâshim from Quraish, and He chose me from Banu Hâshim."

**Source: At-Tirmidhî**

سورة قريش

Ruku': 1

بِسۡمِ اللّٰهِ الرَّحۡمٰنِ الرَّحِيۡمِ

Āyah: 4

لِاِيۡلٰفِ قُرَيۡشٍ ۙ (1) اٖلٰفِهِمۡ رِحۡلَةَ

الشِّتَآءِ وَالصَّيۡفِ ۚ (2) فَلۡيَعۡبُدُوۡا رَبَّ

هٰذَا الۡبَيۡتِ ۙ (3) الَّذِىۡۤ اَطۡعَمَهُمۡ مِّنۡ

جُوۡعٍ ۙ وَّاٰمَنَهُمۡ مِّنۡ خَوۡفٍ (4) ع

ع 1 4 31

Excellent | Good | Repeat

Comments:

I need more help with: Recognition / Articulation / Fluency

Date Started: / /

Date Completed: / /

Read with Ghunnah — Read with Madd (stretch) — Silent letters — Read with Qalqalah (echo) — Read with velerisation (Full Mouth)

**Sayyidinah 'Ali ﷺ narrates that Rasūlullāh ﷺ said:**
**"Whoever reads Qur'ān and learns it by heart, and regards what it makes lawful as lawful and what it makes unlawful as unlawful, will be admitted into Jannah by Almighty Allāh, who will also accept his intercession in respect of ten such persons of his family who would otherwise have gone to Jahannam."**
**Source: At-Tirmidhī**

# Small Kindnesses

Revealed in Makkah

**Order in Mushaf:** 107

**Order in revelation:** 17

## About the Sûrah

Sûrah al-Mã'oon gets its name from the word al-Mã'oon, which means "small acts of kindness" which Allãh ﷻ mentions in the last Âyah. In fact this is one of only a few Sûrahs in the Qur'ãn which are named after their very last word.

Like Sûrah al-Humazah, this Sûrah also warns against some very bad qualities found among people; in this case they are:

i) driving away orphans and acting harshly towards them
ii) refusing to feed the poor
iii) being unmindful of salãh (daily prayers) and praying without concentration
iv) doing things just for show and not because you mean it
v) avoiding all acts of kindness, even very small ones

Importantly, this Sûrah describes people with the above traits as being like those who deny religion, which is a terrible position to be in. Hence we should all ask Allãh ﷻ to help us avoid having any of the above traits in our lives.

## Al-Hadîth

**Sahl bin Sa'd ؓ narrates:**

"Rasulullah ﷺ said 'I and the person who looks after an orphan and provides for him, will be in Paradise like this' and he put his index and middle fingers together [showing how close they will be]."

Source: Al-Bukhãrî

سورة الماعون

Ruku': 1

بِسۡمِ اللّٰهِ الرَّحۡمٰنِ الرَّحِيۡمِ

Āyah: 7

اَرَءَيۡتَ الَّذِىۡ يُكَذِّبُ بِالدِّيۡنِ 1

فَذٰلِكَ الَّذِىۡ يَدُعُّ الۡيَتِيۡمَ 2

وَلَا يَحُضُّ عَلٰى طَعَامِ الۡمِسۡكِيۡنِ 3

فَوَيۡلٌ لِّلۡمُصَلِّيۡنَ 4 الَّذِيۡنَ هُمۡ عَنۡ

صَلَاتِهِمۡ سَاهُوۡنَ 5 الَّذِيۡنَ هُمۡ

يُرَآءُوۡنَ 6 وَيَمۡنَعُوۡنَ الۡمَاعُوۡنَ 7 ع

ع 1 7 32

Excellent
Good
Repeat

Comments:

I need more help with:
Recognition
Articulation
Fluency

Date Started: / /

Date Completed: / /

نّ مّ نۡ ںًّ مۡ — Read with Ghunnah

ــٓ ــٓ ىٓ وٓ ي — Read with Madd (stretch)

ا و ي — Silent letters

قۡ طۡ بۡ جۡ دۡ — Read with Qalqalah (echo)

ظ ط ض ص ق غ خ رُ — Read with velerisation (Full Mouth)

# The Abundance

Order in Mushaf: **108**

Order in revelation: **15**



## About the Sûrah

Sûrah al-Kawthar gets its name from the word al-Kawthar, which is mentioned in the first Âyah. "Al-Kawthar" has several meanings, all of which can be conveyed by the idea of 'An Abundance Of Good'. The word also refers to a special river in Paradise which has been given to Rasullullâh ﷺ,and from which his Ummah will quench their thirst, Inshâ'-Allâh.

Sûrah al-Kawthar was revealed after Rasûlullâh's ﷺ young son died in infancy and his enemies started rejoicing and taunting him. The Sûrah promises Rasûlullâh ﷺ,and therefore his followers as well, an abundance of good things in this world and the hereafter. In return we are asked to perform our Salâh and give up those things which Allâh ﷻ has asked us to.

Sûrah al-Kawthar has the distinction of being the shortest Sûrah in the Qur'ân, yet it remains one of the most powerful and affecting.

## Al-Hadîth

Anas رضي الله عنه narrates:

"While we were with Rasûlullâh ﷺ in the masjid he dozed off into a slumber. Then he lifted his head smiling. We asked, 'O Rasûlullâh ﷺ what has caused you to smile?' He replied 'Verily, a Sûrah was just revealed to me'. Then he recited Sûrah al-Kawthar and said "By this book [the Qur'ân], Allâh would exalt [to a high status] some peoples and degrade others."

Source: Muslim

# سورة الكوثر

Ruku': 1

# بِسۡمِ اللّٰهِ الرَّحۡمٰنِ الرَّحِيۡمِ

Āyah: 3

1 اِنَّاۤ اَعۡطَيۡنٰكَ الۡكَوۡثَرَ

2 فَصَلِّ لِرَبِّكَ وَانۡحَرۡ

3 اِنَّ شَانِئَكَ هُوَ الۡاَبۡتَرُ ع

ع 1 3 33



Excellent ◯
Good ◯
Repeat ◯

Comments:

I need more help with:
Recognition ◯
Articulation ◯
Fluency ◯

Date Started: / /

Date Completed: / /

Read with Ghunnah: نّ مّ ن ـًـٍـٌ م
Read with Madd (stretch): ي و ا ـآ ـٓ
Silent letters: ا و ي
Read with Qalqalah (echo): قْ طْ بْ جْ دْ
Read with velerisation (Full Mouth): ظ ط ض ص ق غ خ رُ

**Abu Musā Al-'Ash'arī narrates that Rasūlullāh said:**

**"The example of a believer who recites the Qur'ān is like that of an Utruj (a fragrant citrus fruit) which both tastes AND smells good, whereas a believer who does not recite the Qur'ān is like a date which is good in taste but has no smell. And the example of a wicked person who recites the Qur'ān is like the Raihana (sweet basil) which smells good but tastes bitter, whereas the example of a wicked person who does not recite the Qur'ān is like the Colocynth (bitter apple) which tastes bitter and has no smell."**

**Source: Al-Bukhārī**

# The Deniers

**Order in Mushaf:** 109

**Order in revelation:** 18

## About the Sûrah

Sûrah al-Kâfiroon gets its name from the word al-Kâfiroon which means "those who deny or reject faith", and which is found in the first Âyah.

The Sûrah discusses how Muslims should reply to those who deny the religion of Allâh and who might encourage Muslims to alter their beliefs.

The Sûrah was revealed after some of the idol-worshippers suggested a compromise to Rasûlullâh ﷺ in which both parties would worship each others' way for a year. Sûrah al-Kâfiroon shows that this is not possible. While Islam is indeed a religion of tolerance and teaches that no-on can be compelled to believe, it also makes clear that its teachings cannot be compromised either.

Sûrah al-Kâfiroon is the first of four Sûrahs often called 'the Four Quls' after their first word, which means 'Say'. All four provide us with a set of words which Allâh ﷻ wants us to recite regularly.

## Al-Hadîth

Nawfal al-Ashja'î narrates that Rasûlullâh ﷺ said to him:

"Recite 'Qul yâ ayyu hal-Kâfiroon' then go to sleep at the end of it, for it is a disavowal of shirk."

Source: At-Tirmidhî

سورة الكافرون

Ruku': 1

# بِسۡمِ اللّٰهِ الرَّحۡمٰنِ الرَّحِيۡمِ

Ayah: 6

1 قُلۡ يٰۤاَيُّهَا الۡكٰفِرُوۡنَ

2 لَاۤ اَعۡبُدُ مَا تَعۡبُدُوۡنَ

3 وَلَاۤ اَنۡتُمۡ عٰبِدُوۡنَ مَاۤ اَعۡبُدُ

4 وَلَاۤ اَنَاۡ عَابِدٌ مَّا عَبَدۡتُّمۡ

5 وَلَاۤ اَنۡتُمۡ عٰبِدُوۡنَ مَاۤ اَعۡبُدُ

6 لَكُمۡ دِيۡنُكُمۡ وَلِىَ دِيۡنِ ع

ع 1 6 34



Excellent
Good
Repeat

Comments:

I need more help with:
Recognition
Articulation
Fluency

Date Started: / /

Date Completed: / /

Read with Ghunnah — Read with Madd (stretch) — Silent letters — Read with Qalqalah (echo) — Read with velerisation (Full Mouth)

**Jābir bin 'Abdullah ﷺ narrates:**
**During the two Raka'ah of Tawāf, Rasūlullāh ﷺ recited the two Sūrahs of Ikhlās, "Say: O you disbelievers!" and "Say: He is Allāh, [the] One."**
**Source: At-Tirmidhī**

# Assistance

**Order in Mushaf:** 110

**Order in revelation:** 114

## About the Sûrah

Sûrah an-Nasr gets its name from the word an-Nasr, which means "help" or "assistance" and which is mentioned in the first Âyah.

Sûrah an-Nasr was the last complete Sûrah to be revealed, and marked the completion of Rasûlullâh's ﷺ mission, as it was revealed after Islam had established itself as a great success, with most of Arabia becoming Muslim and people rushing to accept the religion in huge numbers. This was a time of great rejoicing for the Muslims but also foreshadowed the sadness to come as, shortly after this Sûrah was revealed, in the year 10AH, Rasûlullâh ﷺ passed away and returned to Allâh ﷻ.

The Sûrah reminds us that when Allâh's ﷻ help arrives (as it always surely will) we should remain mindful of the One who granted that help. We should glorify Him and praise Him and continue to seek His forgiveness and protection.

## Al-Hadîth

'Aa'ishah رضي الله عنها narrates that:

"After the revelation of Sûrah an-Nasr, the Messenger of Allâh ﷺ used to recite [the following] in every [ruku' and sajdah]:
'Subhânaka Rabbanâ wa bihamdika, Allâhum-maghfir lî'
(Far removed are You from every imperfection, our Lord, and all praise is for You, forgive me, O Allâh)."

Source: Al-Bukhârî

سورة النصر

Ruku': 1 بِسۡمِ اللّٰهِ الرَّحۡمٰنِ الرَّحِيۡمِ Āyah: 3

اِذَا جَآءَ نَصۡرُ اللّٰهِ وَالۡفَتۡحُ ① وَرَاَيۡتَ

النَّاسَ يَدۡخُلُوۡنَ فِىۡ دِيۡنِ اللّٰهِ

اَفۡوَاجًا ② فَسَبِّحۡ بِحَمۡدِ رَبِّكَ

وَاسۡتَغۡفِرۡهُ ؕ اِنَّهٗ كَانَ تَوَّابًا ③ ع

STOP or CONTINUE

ع 1 3 35

110 - The Assistance

| Excellent | Comments: | I need more help with: | Date Started: / / |
|---|---|---|---|
| Good | | Recognition | Date Completed: / / |
| Repeat | | Articulation | |
| | | Fluency | |

Read with Ghunnah: مٌ ـنّ ن مّ نّ
Read with Madd (stretch): ـــ ـِيْ ـَا ـُو ـِي
Silent letters: ا و ي
Read with Qalqalah (echo): قْ طْ بْ جْ دْ
Read with velerisation (Full Mouth): ظ ط ض ص ق غ خ رُ

مَا شَاءَ اللّٰه
You have just learnt another Sūrah from Al-Qur'ān

Don't forget to mark off on the progress sheet!

**Ibn Mas'ood narrates that Rasūlullāh said:**

"Whoever reads one letter of the Book of Allāh is credited with one blessing and one blessing is equal to tenfold the like thereof in its reward. I do not say that 'الم' (Alif Lām Mīm) is one letter, but 'ا' (Alif) is one letter, 'ل' (Lām) is one letter and 'م' (Mīm) is one letter."

**Source: At-Tirmidhī**

# The Palm Fibre

**Order in Mushaf:** 111

**Order in revelation:** 6

## About the Sûrah

Sûrah al-Masad gets its name from the word al-Masad, which means "The Palm Fibre" which is the last word of the last Âyah (making this one of the few Sûrahs named after its final word). It is also known as Sûrah al-Lahab after Abu Lahab, the uncle of Rasûlullâh ﷺ who is the main subject of the Sûrah.

Although he was Rasûlullâh's ﷺ uncle, Abu-Lahab (whose real name was 'Abdul 'Uzzâ) was a staunch enemy of Islam, the Muslims and the Prophet ﷺ did all he could to oppose them and harm them. In this he was joined by his wife who acted as his accomplice. Sûrah al-Masad discusses the fate of these two people but also carries the wider message that we will all have to face the consequences of our actions in the âkhirah, whether we are the instigator or an accomplice.

The Sûrah also mentions that Abu Lahab's wealth, the source of his power and influence, will be of no benefit to him in the hereafter, reminding us once again that possessions and position in this world are transitory.

المسد

## Al-Hadîth

**Rabi'ah bin Abbâs ؓ narrates that:**

"I saw Rasûlullâh ﷺ ...in the market...saying 'O people! Say there is no god worthy of worship except Allâh, and you will be successful' and behind him there was a man with a bright face, a squint and two braids in his hair. He was saying 'Verily he [The Prophet ﷺ] is an apostate and a liar.' This man was following him [The Prophet ﷺ] around wherever he went. I asked who he was and the people said 'This is his uncle, Abu Lahab.' "

**Source: Musnad of Imâm Ahmad**

سورة المسد

Ruku': 1

بِسۡمِ اللّٰهِ الرَّحۡمٰنِ الرَّحِيۡمِ

Āyah: 5

تَبَّتۡ يَدَاۤ اَبِىۡ لَهَبٍ وَّتَبَّ ﴿1﴾ مَاۤ اَغۡنٰى

عَنۡهُ مَالُهٗ وَمَا كَسَبَ ﴿2﴾ سَيَصۡلٰى نَارًا

ذَاتَ لَهَبٍ ﴿3﴾ وَّامۡرَاَتُهٗ حَمَّالَةَ الۡحَطَبِ

﴿4﴾ فِىۡ جِيۡدِهَا حَبۡلٌ مِّنۡ مَّسَدٍ ﴿5﴾ ع

ع 1 5 36

Excellent | Good | Repeat

Comments:

I need more help with: Recognition ○ Articulation ○ Fluency ○

Date Started: / /

Date Completed: / /

Read with Ghunnah | Read with Madd (stretch) | Silent letters | Read with Qalqalah (echo) | Read with velerisation (Full Mouth)



مَا شَاءَ اللّٰه
You have just learnt another Sūrah from Al-Qur'ān

Don't forget to mark off on the progress sheet!

'Aa'ishah narrates that Rasūlullāh said:
"Whoever recites the Qur'ān and masters it by heart, will be with the 'noble righteous scribes', i.e the messenger Angels [in Heaven]. Moreover, whoever recites the Qur'ān and stutters with it, or has difficulty, will receive a double reward."
Source: Muslim

# Sincerity

Revealed in Makkah

Order in Mushaf: **112**

Order in revelation: **22**

## About the Sûrah

Sûrah al-Ikhlâs, gets its name from the Arabic word for "sincerity" although the word itself does not appear within the Sûrah. Instead it indicates the sincerity with which we should believe and hold firm to the central message of the verses, which is that of 'tawheed": the Oneness of Allâh. Hence, it is also known as Surah at-Tawheed" (The Unity).

Sûrah al-Ikhlâs is the second of the 'Four Quls', the Sûrahs which begin with the word 'Qul' or 'Say...' because they tell us to recite the words that follow. In this Sûrah the words are:

"Say: He is Allâh the One;
Allâh, the Eternal and Self-Sufficient
He does not beget (have children), nor is He begotten (have parents)
And there is nothing else like or equal to Him"

This is perhaps the most important and powerful message in creation, yet it is encompassed within a Sûrah so short that it is easy for everyone to memorise. Thus we should all learn it by heart and recite it as often as possible. Rasûlullâh ﷺ recommended that we should recite it three times in the morning and evening, and before we make duâ.

## Al-Hadîth

Abu Sa'eed Al-Khudri narrates that Rasûlullâh ﷺ once said to his companions:

"Rasûlullâh ﷺ once said to his companions 'Is it difficult for any of you to recite one third of the Qur'ân in one night?' This suggestion was difficult for them so they said, 'Who among us has the power to do so, O Rasûlullâh ﷺ?' Rasûlullâh ﷺ replied: 'Sûrah Al-Ikhlâs is equal to one third of the Qur'ân.' "

Source: Al-Bukhârî

# سورة الإخلاص

Ruku': 1 بِسۡمِ اللّٰهِ الرَّحۡمٰنِ الرَّحِيۡمِ Āyah: 4

قُلۡ هُوَ اللّٰهُ اَحَدٌ ۚ (1) اَللّٰهُ الصَّمَدُ ۚ (2)

لَمۡ يَلِدۡ وَلَمۡ يُوۡلَدۡ ۙ (3)

وَلَمۡ يَكُنۡ لَّهٗ كُفُوًا اَحَدٌ (4) ع

ع 1 4 37

| | | | |
|---|---|---|---|
| Excellent / Good / Repeat | Comments: | I need more help with: Recognition / Articulation / Fluency | Date Started: / / <br> Date Completed: / / |

Read with Ghunnah · Read with Madd (stretch) · Silent letters · Read with Qalqalah (echo) · Read with velerisation (Full Mouth)

مَا شَاءَ اللّٰه
You have just learnt another Sūrah from Al-Qur'ān

Don't forget to mark off on the progress sheet!

**'Abdullāh ibn 'Amr narrates that Rasūlullāh said:**
**"On the Day of Judgement, it will be said to the devotee of the Qur'ān 'Ascend the storeys of Paradise and keep reciting the Qur'ān in the same slow manner in which you used to read during your worldly life. You will continue to ascend the levels of Paradise until you reach the final Ayāh of your recitation' "**

**Source: At-Tirmidhī**

# Daybreak

Al-Mu’awwadhatayn

Order in Mushaf: **113**

Order in revelation: **20**

## About the Sûrah

Sûrah al-Falaq gets its name from the word al-Falaq, which means “Daybreak”, mentioned in the first Âyah.
It is the third of the ‘Qul’ Sûrahs in which Allâh ﷻ asks us to recite the words that follow. This Sûrah and the next are also called ‘Al-Mu'awwadhatayn’, the Sûrahs of Protection, because Rasûlullâh ﷺ told us that they should be recited to protect us against all kinds of dangers.

The words of Sûrah al-Falaq seek protection in Allâh ﷻ, the One who turns night to day (i.e brings light out of darkness). It also specifically seeks protection from i) all kinds of evil or danger that might exist in Allâh’s ﷻ vast creation. ii) the spread and increase of ‘darkness’ in all areas of life, such as the darkness of poverty, superstition and ignorance. iii) people who claim to practice magic and cast spells, and iv) the evil of envy, including ones own envy and that of envious people.

## Al-Hadîth

’Aa’îshah ؓ narrated that:
“Whenever Rasûlullâh ﷺ became sick, he would recite Al-Mu’awwadhatayn (Sûrah al-Falaq and Sûrah an-Nâs) and then blow his breath over his body. When he became seriously ill, I used to recite [these two Sûrahs] and rub his hands over his body, hoping for their blessings.”
Source: Al-Bukhârî

سورة الفلق

Ruku': 1

# بِسۡمِ اللّٰهِ الرَّحۡمٰنِ الرَّحِيۡمِ

Āyah: 5

قُلۡ اَعُوۡذُ بِرَبِّ الۡفَلَقِ ﴿1﴾ مِنۡ شَرِّ مَا

خَلَقَ ﴿2﴾ وَمِنۡ شَرِّ غَاسِقٍ اِذَا وَقَبَ ﴿3﴾

وَمِنۡ شَرِّ النَّفّٰثٰتِ فِى الۡعُقَدِ ﴿4﴾

وَمِنۡ شَرِّ حَاسِدٍ اِذَا حَسَدَ ﴿5﴾ ع

ع 1 5 38

| Excellent | Comments: | I need more help with: | Date Started: / / |
|---|---|---|---|
| Good | | Recognition | Date Completed: / / |
| Repeat | | Articulation | |
| | | Fluency | |

Read with Ghunnah · Read with Madd (stretch) · Silent letters · Read with Qalqalah (echo) · Read with velerisation (Full Mouth)

مَا شَاءَ اللّٰه
You have just learnt another Sūrah from Al-Qur'ān

Don't forget to mark off on the progress sheet!

**Abu 'Umāmah narrates that Rasūlullāh said:**
**"Recite the Qur'ān, for it comes on the Day of Resurrection as an intercessor for the one who carries it [in his heart and in his actions]".**
**Source: Muslim**

# Humankind

Al-Mu'awwadhatayn

Revealed in Makkah

Order in Mushaf: **114**

Order in revelation: **21**



## About the Sûrah

Sûrah an-Nâs gets its name from the word an-Nâs, which means "Humankind" which Allâh ﷻ mentions at the end of the first Âyah, but also at the end of four of the other five Âyahs, making it the only Surah which has the same word ending in all but one verse. This is the fourth of the 'Four Quls', the Sûrahs which begin with the word 'Qul' meaning 'Say...' because Allâh wants us to repeat the words that follow. It is also the second of the two 'Al-Mu'awwadhatayn', the Sûrahs of Protection.

While Sûrah al-Falaq seeks protection from Allâh's creation in general, Sûrah an-Nâs seeks protection specifically from the evil of human beings and Jinn, by beseeching the One who is the Lord and Master of all humans and Jinn. It also specifically seeks protection from those human and Jinn who whisper evil and temptation into the hearts of human beings.

And lastly, Sûrah an-Nâs is the 114th and final Sûrah of the whole Glorious Qur'ân, and it is a testament to Allâh's great mercy that He ends His book with two Sûrahs that protect the reciter.

## Al-Hadîth

'Aa'ishah رضي الله عنها narrates that:

"Whenever Rasûllullâh ﷺ went to bed at night, he used to cup his hands together and blow into them after reciting Sûrah al-Ikhlâs, Sûrah al-Falaq and Sûrah an-Nâs, and then rub his hands over whatever parts of his body he was able to rub, starting with his head, face and the front of his body. He used to do this three times."

Source: Al-Bukhârî

سورة الناس

Ruku': 1 بِسۡمِ اللّٰهِ الرَّحۡمٰنِ الرَّحِيۡمِ Āyah: 6

قُلۡ اَعُوۡذُ بِرَبِّ النَّاسِ ﴿1﴾ مَلِكِ النَّاسِ

﴿2﴾ اِلٰهِ النَّاسِ ﴿3﴾ مِنۡ شَرِّ الۡوَسۡوَاسِ

الۡخَنَّاسِ ﴿4﴾ الَّذِىۡ يُوَسۡوِسُ فِىۡ صُدُوۡرِ

النَّاسِ ﴿5﴾ مِنَ الۡجِنَّةِ وَالنَّاسِ ﴿6﴾ ع

ع 1 6 39

الجزء End of the Juz

114 - Humankind

Excellent | Good | Repeat

Comments:

I need more help with: Recognition, Articulation, Fluency

Date Started: / /

Date Completed: / /

Read with Ghunnah | Read with Madd (stretch) | Silent letters | Read with Qalqalah (echo) | Read with velerisation (Full Mouth)

صدق الله العظيم

مَا شَاءَ اللّٰه You have just learnt another Sūrah from Al-Qur'ān

Don't forget to mark off on the progress sheet!

# الدُّعَاء

اللّٰهُمَّ ارْحَمْنِي بِالْقُرْآنِ الْعَظِيمِ

وَاجْعَلْهُ لِي إِمَامًا وَّنُورًا وَّهُدًى وَّرَحْمَةً

اللّٰهُمَّ ذَكِّرْنِي مِنْهُ مَا نَسِيتُ وَعَلِّمْنِي

مِنْهُ مَا جَهِلْتُ وَارْزُقْنِي تِلَاوَتَهُ آنَاءَ اللَّيْلِ

وَآنَاءَ النَّهَارِ وَاجْعَلْهُ لِي حُجَّةً

يَا رَبَّ الْعَالَمِينَ

**O Allāh! Let me receive Your mercy by means of the Noble Qur'ān and make it my model as well as a source of light, guidance and grace for me.**

**O Allāh! Revive my memory of whatever I was made to forget from the Noble Qur'ān; grant me understanding of whatever part I know not, enable me to recite it during the hours of the day and night, and make it my defensive support (in all matters),**

**O Nourisher of the worlds**

# مَا شَاءَ اللّٰه

# Congratulations

## on

# Completing

## Simple Steps In Qur'ān Reading

# Juz 'Amm

# Section 2

القرآن

Progress

# SŪRAH MEMORISATION PROGRESS CHART

Chapter 1: al-Fâtihah — سورة الفاتحة

Chapter 78: an-Nabâ' — سورة النبأ

Chapter 79: an-Nâzi'ât — سورة النازعات

Chapter 80: 'Abas — سورة عبس

Chapter 81: at-Takweer — سورة التكوير

Chapter 82: al-Infitâr — سورة الإنفطار

Chapter 83: al-Mutaffifeen — سورة المطففين

Chapter 84: al-Inshiqâq — سورة الإنشقاق

Chapter 85: al-Burûj — سورة البروج

Chapter 86: at-Târiq — سورة الطارق

Chapter 87: al-'A'lâ — سورة الأعلى

Chapter 88: al-Ghâshiyah — سورة الغاشية

Chapter 89: al-Fajr — سورة الفجر

# SŪRAH MEMORISATION PROGRESS CHART

Chapter 90 al-Balad — سورة البلد

Chapter 91: ash-Shams — سورة الشمس

Chapter 92: al-Layl — سورة الليل

Chapter 93: ad-Dhuhā — سورة الضحى

Chapter 94: ash-Sharh — سورة الشرح

Chapter 95: at-Teen — سورة التين

Chapter 96: al-'Alaq — سورة العلق

Chapter 97: al-Qadr — سورة القدر

Chapter 98: al-Bayyinah — سورة البينة

Chapter 99: az-Zalzalah — سورة الزلزلة

Chapter 100: al-'Âdiyaat — سورة العاديات

Chapter 101: al-Qāri'ah — سورة القارعة

Chapter 102: at-Takāthur — سورة التكاثر

# SŪRAH MEMORISATION PROGRESS CHART

Chapter 103: al-'Asr — سورة العصر

Chapter 104: al-Humazah — سورة الهمزة

Chapter 105: al-Fīl — سورة الفيل

Chapter 106: Quraish — سورة قريش

Chapter 107: al-Mā'oon — سورة الماعون

Chapter 108: al-Kawthar — سورة الكوثر

Chapter 109: al-Kāfiroon — سورة الكافرون

Chapter 110: an-Nasr — سورة النصر

Chapter 111: al-Masad — سورة المسد

Chapter 112: al-Ikhlās — سورة الإخلاص

Chapter 113: al-Falaq — سورة الفلق

Chapter 114: an-Nās — سورة الناس

Bifadlillāh, Juz 'Amm Completed — بفضل لله نهاية جزء عم

# Section 3

القرآن

# Revision

# SŪRAH REVISION

| | | | | | | | | | | | | |
|---|---|---|---|---|---|---|---|---|---|---|---|---|
| 13 الفجر al-Fajr | | | | | | | | | | | | |
| 12 الغاشية al-Ghâshiyah | | | | | | | | | | | | |
| 11 الأعلى al-'A'lâ | | | | | | | | | | | | |
| 10 الطارق at-Târiq | | | | | | | | | | | | |
| 9 البروج al-Burûj | | | | | | | | | | | | |
| 8 الانشقاق al-Inshiqâq | | | | | | | | | | | | |
| 7 المطففين al-Mutaffifeen | | | | | | | | | | | | |
| 6 الانفطار al-Infitâr | | | | | | | | | | | | |
| 5 التكوير at-Takweer | | | | | | | | | | | | |
| 4 عبس 'Abas | | | | | | | | | | | | |
| 3 النازعات an-Nâzi'ât | | | | | | | | | | | | |
| 2 النبأ an-Nabâ' | | | | | | | | | | | | |
| 1 الفاتحة al-Fâtihah | | | | | | | | | | | | |

# SŪRAH REVISION

| 26 | 25 | 24 | 23 | 22 | 21 | 20 | 19 | 18 | 17 | 16 | 15 | 14 |
|---|---|---|---|---|---|---|---|---|---|---|---|---|
| التكاثر at-Takāthur | القارعة al-Qāri'ah | العاديات al-'Ādiyaat | الزلزلة az-Zalzalah | البينة al-Bayyinah | القدر al-Qadr | العلق al-'Alaq | التين at-Teen | الشرح ash-Sharh | الضحى ad-Dhuhā | الليل al-Layl | الشمس ash-Shams | البلد al-Balad |

# SŪRAH REVISION

| 38 الناس an-Nās | 37 الفلق al-Falaq | 36 الإخلاص al-Ikhlāṣ | 35 المسد al-Masad | 34 النصر an-Naṣr | 33 الكافرون al-Kāfiroon | 32 الكوثر al-Kawthar | 31 الماعون al-Mā'oon | 30 قريش Quraish | 29 الفيل al-Fīl | 28 الهمزة al-Humazah | 27 العصر al-'Asr |
|---|---|---|---|---|---|---|---|---|---|---|---|
| | | | | | | | | | | | |
| | | | | | | | | | | | |
| | | | | | | | | | | | |
| | | | | | | | | | | | |
| | | | | | | | | | | | |
| | | | | | | | | | | | |
| | | | | | | | | | | | |
| | | | | | | | | | | | |
| | | | | | | | | | | | |
| | | | | | | | | | | | |
| | | | | | | | | | | | |
| | | | | | | | | | | | |

# Notes

# المعلومات الشخصية
# PERSONAL INFORMATION

**Name:** الإسم :

**Address:** العنوان:

**School:** إسم المدرسة:

**Class:** القسم :

**Form/Year:** السنة:

**Teacher:** المعلم :

**Date Started:** تاريخ البداية:

**Date Completed:** تاريخ النهاية:

# Important Notes

While using this book, please note the following points:

## Translation/commentary

For each Sûrah we have highlighted some key aspects of the Sûrah's meaning, history, or virtues, rather than necessarily translating or summarising the whole Sûrah. The aim is to distinguish each Sûrah and make it memorable, but without burdening the reader with too much information at this stage. Please consult a good translation and tafseer of the Glorious Qur'ân, with the help of a scholar, for full translations, interpretations and more information.

In terms of translation and tafseer we have stuck to those of Ibn Kathîr as far as possible.

## Style and script

The Arabic script used in this book follows the Uthmâni rasm (orthography), and the Persian/'Ajmi style and font, and conforms to the riwâyah (reading) of Imâm Hafs an Âsim. It is based on either the popular 13-Line South African print or the new 13-Line Darussalam print of the Glorious Qur'ân, or both.

## Stop signs

For ease of use, stop signs are based on the far simpler Madinah Mushaf convention. This means there are fewer stop signs to remember. The function of the stop sign has also been written in English above the sign.

## Tajweed and colour-coding

This book uses a colour-coded script to indicate tajweed rules and help facilitate correct recitation of the Qurân. This method is particularly effective because it engages the eye and confers tajweed information as part of the normal reading process. Thus all reading becomes tajweed practice and eventually the reader can do without the colour-coding, Inshâ' Allâh.

Rather than give each distinct tajweed rule its own colour, letters have been classified into one of five categories of tajweed, each category containing all similar and related rules. The categories are:

| | |
|---|---|
| BLUE | Letters which require velarisation (full mouth pronunciation) |
| GREEN | Letters which should be pronounced nasally |
| RED | Letters which need to be elongated |
| BLUE | Letters which need to be pronounced with a slight reverberation |
| GREY | Letters which should not be pronounced and should be silent |

Full explanations of every tajweed rule have NOT been included in this book as it is assumed readers will have the necessarily basic knowledge. For more information on each tajweed rule, please consult the SSiQR Introductory Tajweed guide or check with a qualified Qâri' or scholar.

Where a letter has two tajweed attributes, which are ordinarily indicated by different colours, the most appropriate of the two has been chosen in each instance, based on position and context.

The word Allâh has been colour-coded in gold in two ways: a darker shade indicates the need for velaraisation, while the lighter shade indicates no velarisation.

For colour-coding purposes it has been assumed that the reader is starting at the start of an Âyah and stopping at the end (i.e no continuations, for which different rules may apply). In practice this means there's no colour-coding at the end of Âyahs.

Please note that all colour-coding is just for guidance. Please consult a Qur'ân teacher to learn correct pronunciation of letters and tajweed rules.

# AFTERWORD

بسم الله الرحمن الرحيم

الحمد لله الذي علم الإنسان ما لم يعلم والصلوة والسلام على حبيبه محمدﷺأما بعد.....

All praises belong to our Creator and Sustainer, Allāh ﷻ and peace and blessings be upon our Beloved Nabī ﷺ

Tajweed is the art of reading the Glorious Qur'ān using the rules and pronunciation practised by the Noble Prophet ﷺ, and given to him by Allāh Almighty Himself via the Angel Jibreel ؑ. Tajweed is thus an essential part of Qur'ānic recitation, but one which many people regard as complex or difficult and often fail to learn properly. We thank Allāh ﷻ, therefore, for helping us complete this new standalone Edition of Juz 'Amm to add to the successful 'Simple Steps in Qur'ān Reading' series as an optional Part 4 (previously half of the Juz was incorporated into the old Part 3). As the title suggests, with this manual you are only a few Simple Steps away from reading a complete Juz of the Qur'ān with tajweed.

The publication of this optional Part 4 completes the newly structured SSiQR series, with the full Qā'idah forming Parts 1 and 2 and the optional Tajweed guide as Part 3. This ensures that only parts 1 and 2 are now necessary for learning to read the Qur'ān, with the other two parts as optional extras. The whole SSiQR series has thus been professionally restructured, re-edited and redesigned to make it easier to use, more effective and more affordable. We hope you'll find these changes helpful.

Features of the 'Simple Steps in Qur'ān Reading' Juz 'Amm include:

- ☒ All Sūrahs from Juz 'Amm, plus Sūrah al-Fātihah
- ☒ Bright and colourful design, specially developed to make learning fun as well as effective
- ☒ New and improved font which is larger and easier to read for first-time Qur'ān readers
- ☒ Colour-coding of Tajweed (see next page for details)
- ☒ Stop sign functions indicated in English
- ☒ A brief introduction to each Sūrah, highlighting keys aspects, virtues and/or historical information
- ☒ A selected hadīth relating to each Sūrah.
- ☒ Lesson review and 'I Need More Help With' boxes at the end of each Sūrah.
- ☒ Motivational Sūrah Progress Chart to aid memorisation
- ☒ Sūrah Revision Chart to aid revision and memorisation

Although we have taken every care in the compilation and production of this book, please contact us should you find any errors or omissions, or if you have any comments. Your feedback is always welcome.
May Allāh ﷻ forgive my shortcomings and accept this work as a means of acquiring His pleasure and closeness to His beloved Prophet ﷺ. May He reward my family and friends and all well-wishers who have supported and encouraged me in this noble work.

Abu-Saalihah bin Ayyub
Khādim al-Qur'ān
Nuneaton, England
27 Ramadhān al-Mubārak, 1438, 2017

SIMPLE IN QUR'ÂN READING
QÂ'IDAH JUZ 'AMM

Second Edition 1443-2022

PREPARED BY
Abu-Saalihah Bin Ayyub
Zeenat-Ul-Qur'aan Academy
Nuneaton, England, UK

SERIES EDITOR:
A. A. Ebrahim



ISBN- Paperback: 978-1-911314-15-8
Hardback: 978-1-911314-08-0
A catalogue record of this book is available from the British Library

PUBLISHED BY

Wisdom PUBLICATIONS

© WISDOM PUBLICATIONS
info@wisdompublications.co.uk
www.wisdompublications.co.uk

DESIGN AND PAGE SETTING:
Abu-Saalihah Bin Ayyub UK
Bint Muhammad-Asif Bin Ayyub UK

Printed by imak ofset, Turkey

الطبعة الأولى ١٤٣٧ هـ - ٢٠١٦ م
الطبعة الثانية ١٤٤٣ هـ - ٢٠٢٢ م

**First Edition** 1437 - 2016
**Second Edition** 1443 - 2022

This new edition of Juz 'Amm is dedicated to my dear friend and mentor Shaykh Qārī Abbas bin Ishaq Rahīmahullāh who sadly passed away just before Ramadhān al-Mubārak 1438/2017.

Shaykh Abbas was present at the very start of all my work on the SSiQR series, and the establishment of Zeenatul Qur'ān Academy and Wisdom Publications, and his initial encouragement and constant support was essential for all that has followed. Inshā'-Allāh he is reaping the rewards of everything that we have achieved since then.
May Allāh grant him the highest abode in Jannah and grant his family and friends patience and comfort.

PUBLISHED BY:

Wisdom
PUBLICATIONS

info@wisdompublications.co.uk
www.wisdompublications.co.uk